1968

1968

Michael T. Kaufman

A *New York Times* Book

Roaring Brook Press • New York

Rb.
*Flash
Point*

Text copyright © 2009 by *The New York Times*

Flash Point is an imprint of Roaring Brook Press, a division
of Holtzbrinck Publishing Holdings Limited Partnership.

175 Fifth Avenue, New York, New York 10010

All rights reserved

Jacket and book design by Edward Miller

Photo research by Maggie Berkvist

Library of Congress Cataloging-in-Publication Data

Kaufman, Michael T.

  1968 / Michael T. Kaufman. — 1st ed.

    p. cm.

  "A *New York Times* book."

  Includes bibliographical references and index.

   ISBN-13: 978-1-59643-428-8 (hbk.)

   ISBN-10: 1-59643-428-7 (hbk.)

  1. Nineteen sixty-eight, A.D. I. Title.

  D848.K37 2008

  909.82'6—dc22

                2008015471

Roaring Brook Press books are available for special promotions and premiums.

For details contact: Director of Special Markets, Holtzbrinck Publishers.

Printed in China

First Edition January 2009

1 2 3 4 5 6 7 8 9 10

To my grandchildren,
Zipporah, Hilary, Boaz,
Theo, Reuben, and Aaron

January 5

Alexander Dubček becomes first secretary of the Communist Party in Czechoslovakia. Over the following months he will loosen restrictions and allow greater personal expression during a period later called the "Prague Spring."

31

The Tet Offensive, a notoriously bloody military campaign, is launched in Vietnam. In less than two months, the death toll will reach roughly 56,000.

February 1

A Vietcong officer is executed in Saigon by South Vietnamese officer Nguyen Ngoc Loan. Photos of the execution make headlines, and help sway many Americans against the war.

29

The Kerner Commission—a national commission appointed by President Lyndon B. Johnson to investigate the causes of race riots that broke out in 1967—releases its findings. The report cites systematic racial discrimination in the United States as the cause of the unrest.

March 12

Eugene McCarthy's strong showing in the New Hampshire Presidential primary shows that the incumbent, Lyndon Johnson, is vulnerable.

16

U.S. troops massacre villagers at My Lai.

Robert Kennedy enters the presidential race.

9

Student radical Mark Rudd seizes the microphone at a service for Dr. King at Columbia University to criticize the school's administration, setting the stage for demonstrations on the New York City campus.

11

Lyndon Johnson signs the Civil Rights Act of 1968.

23

Columbia students rally and occupy school buildings for eight days.

18

The U.S. State Department announces highest casualty rate of Vietnam War, with 543 Americans killed the previous week.

24

Tet Offensive is halted as South Vietnamese troops retake Hue.

27

Walter Cronkite delivers a speech in which he states that it is clear to him the U.S. is mired in a stalemate in Vietnam and should seek to negotiate a way out.

22

Led by Daniel Cohn-Bendit, five hundred French students seize a faculty lounge at the University of Nanterre, Paris, and occupy it overnight.

31

Lyndon Johnson delivers a speech announcing his decision not to seek reelection.

April 4

Martin Luther King, Jr., is shot in Memphis, prompting a manhunt for gunman James Earl Ray, and sparking riots in many major American cities.

29

Police storm Columbia University at two A.M., forcibly bringing an end to the student occupation.

May 2

Cohn-Bendit receives a summons to appear before a disciplinary board; a subsequent protest ends in six hundred arrests and the temporary closing of the university.

6

The day of the Cohn-Bendit hearing, street fighting erupts between student protesters and the Paris police.

13

A one-day general strike in support of students brings France to a halt.

31

More than 300,000 workers participate in a union-led march through Paris.

June 5

Robert Kennedy is shot and mortally wounded; he dies the next day after having won the hotly contested California primary.

8

Richard Milhous Nixon is nominated as the presidential candidate for the Republican Party.

20

Alexander Dubček is removed to a KGB stronghold as Soviet forces invade Czechoslovakia, crushing the "Prague Spring."

27

Alexander Dubček returns to Prague and soon after is ousted from the Communist Party, as actions are taken to restore censorship.

18

Armored vehicles surround the main campus of the National Autonomous University of Mexico. As many as 1,000 students and teachers are arrested.

23

Mexican police and army invade the national polytechnic institute in Mexico City; students are shot at with at least forty wounded, but the Mexican Press provides scant coverage.

October 2–3

Student demonstrators are massacred at Tlatelolco Square in Mexico. At least 20 are killed, but estimates range as high as 325.

November 4

Richard Nixon is elected as the thirty-seventh U.S. president, with Spiro Agnew as vice president.

14

"National Turn in Your Draft Card Day" features draft card burning.

21

The Apollo 8 mission to orbit the moon is launched.

8

James Earl Ray is arrested for the murder of Martin Luther King, Jr.

July 16

Police retake the Sorbonne, which had been seized by students following the general strike in France.

August 2

First Secretary Dubček addresses the Czech people in an attempt to dispel rumors of menacing Soviet troop movements.

28

As many watch on television, Chicago police attack protesters in the streets outside the Democratic National Convention.

29

After a contentious convention, divided Democrats nominate Lyndon B. Johnson's vice president, Hubert H. Humphrey, as their presidential candidate.

September 7

Picketers in Atlantic City burn bras to protest the Miss America beauty contest.

12

The nineteenth summer Olympic games open in Mexico City.

Apollo 7, the first manned Apollo mission, is launched from Cape Kennedy.

16

Two American athletes, Tommie Smith and John Carlos, hold up their fists in a salute to black power and unity as they receive Olympic gold and bronze medals for the two-hundred-meter race.

21

President Johnson announces a halt to all U.S. bombing in Vietnam, effective the next morning.

December 24

The world sees itself as never before when the first pictures of Earth taken from the moon are transmitted from the Apollo 8 spacecraft and broadcast widely in the media.

CONTENTS

A YEAR LIKE NO OTHER

As people grow older, it is common for memories of certain years to fade or blur. After a while, the years run together so that it's difficult to remember which grade you were in when something happened, which friend you met first, how you celebrated each birthday, or when exactly you learned to ride a bicycle or swim.

History is very much like that. Over time, some years—maybe even most of them—become fuzzy or indistinct, their events and details merging with our recollections of what happened before and what followed. But there are some years that stand out more clearly than the rest, when in our memory it seems that the world spun faster and that important and unexpected things occurred almost on a daily basis.

1968 was that kind of a year.

That year, tensions that had been building for decades reached a boiling point and spilled over into sudden violent confrontations. Many groups that felt they were being ignored—among them racial and ethnic minorities and women—passionately demanded to be heard. They were joined by millions of teenagers and young adults who found a new and powerful voice.

The kettle had been simmering dangerously for some time. For decades, the civil rights movement had been building across the country. Peaceful activists, following the ideals of leaders such as Martin Luther King, Jr., made increasingly vocal demands for racial equality. Frustration over segregation and discrimination based on race had led some to embrace the Black Power movement, which encouraged an armed, physical response to the problem. In 1967, racially charged conflicts broke out in cities around the United States, including one massive riot in Detroit, which sparked the formation of a congressional commission to determine the cause of the unrest.

A movement to end the war in Vietnam was also growing increasingly frustrated as 1968 approached. The original U.S. commitment to send a few dozen military instructors to Vietnam in 1953 had steadily and sharply increased so

U.S. Marines wait to take part in an attack on Khe Sanh, Vietnam, April 1968.

that by 1968 just about every American knew someone who had been drafted into the military. Also rising sharply were the prominently reported numbers of American troops being killed and wounded. In the end, the total American losses to the war would reach more than 57,000.

The war had an especially profound effect on American teenagers. Local draft boards considered all eighteen-, nineteen-, and twenty-year-old men eligible to fight, though they were not old enough to vote. As the numbers of American troops being killed and wounded rose, opposition to the war and the draft mounted.

On college campuses across the country, a new youth movement galvanized debate. Students and professors held "teach-ins" discussing the origin and conduct of the war. The war had polarized the country. Young men divided into two groups: "hawks" and "doves." Hawks supported the war. Doves represented dissent, antiwar attitudes, and contempt for conventional authority.

Some burned their draft cards or turned them in to the Justice Department, while others made their way to Canada to avoid conscription. The music of the time reflected and propelled a culture increasingly driven by strident and energized youth. Many assembled into or identified with emerging groups whose dress, lifestyle, or slang identified them as "freaks," "flower children," or "hippies." Some were wanderers and others congregated in college towns, merging their antiwar sentiments with hedonistic pursuits stereotypically described under the heading of "sex, drugs, and rock 'n' roll." They flocked to "countercultural" haunts such as coffeehouses or followed their favorite folk musicians or bands on tour, often joining in to sing songs they regarded as contemporary anthems. One of these was a bitterly ironic upbeat tune written and performed by Country Joe McDonald that was called the "I-Feel-Like-I'm-Fixin'-To-Die Rag." It included these lyrics:

> *Yeah, come on all of you, big strong men,*
> *Uncle Sam needs your help again.*
> *He's got himself in a terrible jam*
> *Way down yonder in Vietnam*
> *So put down your books and pick up*
> *   a gun,*
> *We're gonna have a whole lotta fun.*
> *And it's one, two, three,*
> *   What are we fighting for ?*
> *Don't ask me, I don't give a damn,*
> *   Next stop is Vietnam;*
> *And it's five, six, seven,*

Students protest the war on the Columbia University campus, New York, 1968.

Open up the pearly gates,
Well there ain't no time to wonder why,
Whoopee! we're all gonna die.

When I look back at the events that characterized this incredible year, I remember many from the point of view of my job as a *New York Times* reporter. At the start of 1968, I was beginning my third year on rewrite, which was a specialized job on the newspaper staff in the days before word processors, computers, and instantaneous phone and e-mail connections. There were eight of us on duty at *The New York Times* every night, with most starting at six in the evening and working to one in the morning, and two "latemen" starting at seven-thirty and finishing after the paper's final edition was locked up at three A.M.

Our job was to write late-breaking stories. After the other journalists had turned in their stories and gone home for the night, we sat by the phones. If a newsworthy event happened, we scrambled to write it before the paper hit the presses in the morning. We had to research and write very quickly and to be ready for anything—one night I might write an obituary of an opera singer who died on stage, and the next night, outline the history of a country whose leader had just been overthrown. We wrote of hurricanes, floods, earthquakes, and plane crashes, as well as police stories about crimes and arrests. We thought of ourselves as firemen. Like them, we were trained to move quickly whenever alarms went off. But when nothing was happening, we read, played cards or chess, or wrote letters to friends.

I had learned a lot on rewrite, but as 1968 began, I was hoping to move on to become a general assignment reporter. Most of our research on rewrite was done over the phone, and I was anxious to get out on the street. My dream was to one day become a foreign correspondent, and I wanted to prepare for that by directly observing events rather than limiting myself to phone interviews.

But like so many things in 1968, rewrite was also changing. Many of the year's tempestuous events happened at night, so I was often sent out to cover them in person: camping out until dawn in college buildings occupied by angry students, or wandering tense city streets and reporting from the scenes of protests, smelling tear gas and witnessing acts of brutality, fear, and courage. And on the nights when I was at my desk, I followed the chaotic events mushrooming around the world by reading the accounts of *Times* correspondents and wire service reporters. From night rewrite I watched the story of 1968 unfold, all the while trying to understand what the turbulence and turmoil meant.

An antidraft demonstrator outside of a New York City military induction center, July 2, 1968.

PRESIDENT ASKS PAY-PRICE CURBS AND RISE IN TAX

INFLATION FEARED

Economic Report Says Failure to Act Risks a 'Feverish Boom'

Text of Johnson's Economic Report, Pages 20 and 21.

By EDWIN L. DALE Jr.
Special to The New York Times

WASHINGTON, Feb. 1—The Johnson Administration asserted today that there would be "no prospect" of slowing the pace of inflation this year unless negotiated union wage settlements were "appreciably

LINDSAY REDUCES OUTLAY OF FUNDS FOR NEW SCHOOLS

Cites Unused Backlog as He Submits a 'Tight' Capital Budget of $996-Million

Excerpts from capital budget appear on Page 22.

By RICHARD E. MOONEY

Mayor Lindsay submitted a $996-million capital budget yesterday for the coming fiscal year—slightly reduced from the current year's record total, but sharply reduced in the sensitive area of schools.

"This is a tight budget," the Mayor said, adding that he had decided to keep it well under the legal limit for city borrowing. It is also "a realistic budget," he said, because it does not include funds for projects that are not moving fast enough to need money next year, such as school construction.

M'NAMARA SAY SOVIET DOUBL ITS ICBM'S IN

But Secretary, in Far Report, Tells Cong U.S. Force Is Bigge

Excerpts from the McNa report are on Page 1

By WILLIAM BEECH
Special to The New York Time

WASHINGTON, Feb. Soviet Union took a gian toward closing the nucle sile gap last year by mor doubling its force of in tinental ballistic missile fense Secretary Robe McNamara disclosed tod

But the outgoing chief indicated he did gard the development a ticularly ominous. Each he said, now possesses gic forces capable of with ing a surprise attack and ating overwhelmingly the other.

Making it clear that

ork Times

Weather: Rain, mild temperatures today, tonight. Showers tomorrow. Temp. range: today 42-35. Thurs. 36-32. Full U. S. report on Page 70.

FEBRUARY 2, 1968

10 CENTS

STREET CLASHES GO ON IN VIETNAM, FOE STILL HOLDS PARTS OF CITIES; JOHNSON PLEDGES NEVER TO YIELD

January/February 1968

TET

By 1968 the cold war, which divided much of the world into opposing camps, had been building for nearly a quarter of a century. Since World War II, the Soviet Union and the United States had been facing off on literal and symbolic battlegrounds throughout the world. Meanwhile, old European colonial powers had been withdrawing from lands they had ruled on other continents, mostly Asia and Africa. As these newly independent countries sought to find their way, they often became entangled in global rivalry as the planet's two major nuclear powers jockeyed for strategic advantage. That is what had happened in Vietnam, where after the French authorities left, the country was fought over by a largely American-backed force centered in South Vietnam against an opposing North Vietnamese army that received support from the Soviet Union and China.

It had started modestly in 1955 when President Eisenhower had sent a handful of military advisers to help the French there. Since the 1950s, Vietnam had been divided into two parts, with the north led by Ho Chi Minh, a nationalist and Communist who had long struggled both against French colonialism and Japanese occupation in World War II. North Vietnam, with its capital in Hanoi, was supported by Communist China and the Soviet Union. Meanwhile, the southern part of the country, with its capital in Saigon, was ruled by anti-Communists with close ties to France. In 1954, an international agreement reached in Geneva separated Vietnam at the seventeenth parallel and called for nationwide elections on the country's political future. In the next year, South Vietnam, with U.S. backing, refused to participate in elections. From that point on, the conflict kept growing in scale and bitterness, turning into a full-scale civil war with each side backed by nuclear-armed superpowers.

In the early 1960s, during the administration

HO CHI MINH

Among twentieth-century statesmen, Ho Chi Minh was remarkable both for the tenacity and patience with which he pursued his goal of Vietnamese independence and for his success in blending Communism with nationalism.

From his youth Ho espoused freedom for the French colony of Vietnam. He persevered through years when his chances of attaining his objective were so minuscule as to seem ridiculous. Ultimately, he organized the defeat of the French in 1954 in the historic battle of Dienbienphu. This battle, a triumph of guerrilla strategy, came nine years after he was named president of the Democratic Republic of Vietnam.

After the supposed temporary division of Vietnam at the seventeenth parallel by the Geneva Agreement of 1954, and after that division became hardened by the U.S. support of Ngo Dinh Diem in the South, Ho led his countrymen in the North against the onslaughts of American military might. In the war, Ho's capital of Hanoi, among other cities, was repeatedly bombed by American planes.

At the same time, Ho was an inspiration for the National Liberation Front, or Vietcong, which operated in South Vietnam in the long, bloody, and costly conflict against the Saigon regime and its American allies.

In the war, in which the United States became increasingly involved after 1964, Ho maintained an exquisite balance of his relations with the Soviet Union and the People's Republic of China. These Communist countries, at ideological swords' points, were Ho's principal suppliers of foodstuffs and war goods. It was a measure of his diplomacy that he kept on friendly terms with each.

To the 19 million people north of the seventeenth parallel and to other millions below it, the small, frail, ivory-like figure of Ho was that of a patriarch, the George Washington of his nation. Although his name was not attached to public squares, buildings, factories, airports, or monuments, his magnetism was undoubted, as was the affection that the average citizen had for him.

Throughout the Vietnam War, Ho was confident of victory. In 1962, when the war was still a localized conflict between South Vietnamese forces and 11,000 American advisers on the one hand and a smaller guerrilla force on the other, he told a French visitor:

It took us eight years of bitter fighting to defeat your French, and you knew the country and had some old friendships here. Now the South Vietnamese regime is well-armed and helped by the Americans.

The American are much stronger than the French, though they know us less well. So it perhaps may take ten years to do it, but our heroic compatriots in the South will defeat them in the end.

Ho was still confident in early 1967, when he talked with two American journalists. "We have been fighting for our independence for more than twenty-five years," he told them, "and of course we cherish peace, but we will never surrender our independence to purchase a peace with the United States or any party."

of John F. Kennedy, the number of U.S. forces in Vietnam rose to 16,000. By then the French had withdrawn, and the training of the South Vietnamese army was taken over entirely by the United States. When Lyndon Johnson assumed the presidency after John F. Kennedy's assassination in 1963, the deployment of American troops to Vietnam began to rise sharply and then to soar. In 1966, the number more than doubled, jumping from 184,000 to 389,000. By the end of 1967, the total stood at 486,000. In 1968, the number would peak at 537,000.

For most of that time, combat had been waged in rural and remote settings. News accounts, photographs, and television coverage brought images of U.S. soldiers gingerly picking their way through jungles or rice paddies, on the lookout for land mines, booby traps, or ambushes. The dead and wounded could also be seen, fallen combatants from both sides as

Camouflaged Marines on a reconnaissance patrol in Vietnam, February 1968.

well as civilians—men, women, and children. But as the journalist Stanley Karnow noted in his book *Vietnam, a History*, until the end of 1967 television had mostly "transmitted the grueling reality of the struggle—remote, repetitious, monotonous—punctuated periodically by moments of horror."

Early on the morning of January 31, 1968, all of the deliberate plodding came to a sudden, shocking end. That date marked the arrival of Tet, the Vietnamese New Year. Traditionally the weeklong holiday is a time for paying off debts, visiting family, paying respect to ancestors, and appealing for good luck in the forthcoming year. Custom forbids Vietnamese people from mentioning or even thinking about death, so as not to invite any bad fortune. In 1968, as Tet approached, most people in South Vietnam, including American military commanders, presumed the holiday would pass uneventfully, particularly since North Vietnamese leaders in Hanoi had openly declared that they planned to observe a truce during Tet. In light of that promise, South Vietnamese commanders provided furloughs allowing many of their men to go home for the holidays.

But very soon after Tet began, the sound of festive firecrackers was replaced by the menacing clatter of machine guns, mortars, and explosions. The promise of a truce turned out

U.S. marines duck North Vietnamese sniper fire in Hue, February 4, 1968.

to be a North Vietnamese ploy. Trained fighters, who months before had secretly crossed the border from North Vietnam, dug up the guns and ammunition they had hidden and linked up with members of an underground army of Communist fighters based in the south, called the Vietcong. At the appointed moment, they struck in synchronized attacks all over South Vietnam, targeting more than a hundred cities and towns stretching down a 450-mile line from Hue, just below the border separating the two Vietnams, to Saigon, the seemingly impregnable capital near Vietnam's southern end. With the element of surprise on their side, Communist teams invaded thirteen of sixteen provincial capitals in the Mekong Delta and attacked heavily fortified seaside towns that had been considered beyond their range. They even rocketed the enormous port and military installation that the Americans had built at Cam Ranh Bay, where massive shipments of war supplies arrived around the clock.

In many places, the surprise attacks were crushed quickly by the overwhelming military power of American and South Vietnamese units, who struck back furiously with planes, tanks, and artillery. But in other locations, the Northern-led forces dug in and fought with stubborn and brutal resolve. In Hue, a picturesque city of temples and castles, the Communists quickly seized the Citadel, a commanding fortress on high ground. They hoisted the Vietcong flag with its single yellow star and kept it flying for twenty-five days, during which they executed as many as 3,000 residents. Ultimately three battalions of U.S. marines and South Vietnamese troops retook the Citadel and the city in bitter fighting.

In Saigon, North Vietnamese raiders invaded the U.S. embassy. Within minutes of their attack at three A.M. on January 31, they had killed five American soldiers and driven off four Saigon policemen. The U.S. ambassador was awakened and rushed from his residence to spend the night at a less vulnerable site. It was not until nine and a half hours after the initial break-in that U.S. officials were able to declare the embassy secure. Soon after, General William C. Westmoreland, the U.S. military commander in Vietnam, appeared on a televised news conference to accuse the North Vietnamese of acting "very deceitfully." He added that by launching their multipronged offensive, they were seeking "to create maximum consternation," and ended by claiming that his enemies' "well-laid plans went afoul" and that they were "about to run out of steam."

But even as they heard Westmoreland's words, television viewers saw for themselves surprising scenes of carnage and took in the alarming news of Vietcong attacks that had previously seemed unimaginable. In early March, while fighting still continued in certain regions, the U.S. military command reported that throughout the entire combat zone some 2,000 Americans and 4,000 South Vietnamese soldiers had been killed in the month since the Tet Offensive began. At the same time, the Americans declared that the number of enemy troops killed stood at around 50,000.

As people in America and around the world absorbed this news, the realization grew that the daring and ferocity of the countrywide attacks were changing the nature of the war. Nowhere was this more apparent than in Saigon, the sprawling capital where South Vietnam's military and political leaders were concentrated and where the top U.S. military planners and diplomats worked and lived. The city was also home to a large international press corps, and it teemed with reporters and cameramen eager to capture and convey the details and drama of the urban fighting that was suddenly so nearby.

The most enduring image that emerged from Tet was a photograph of just two men, taken on a Saigon street. This image would become one of the most powerful reflections not only of Tet but of the entire Vietnam War. It was taken by Eddie Adams, an Associated Press photographer who was driving slowly through the capital when he noticed a man with his hands tied behind his back being led to a South Vietnamese officer. Adams recognized the officer as General Nguyen Ngoc Loan, the chief of South Vietnam's national police. As Adams focused his camera on the unfolding scene, he shot a sequence of frames that showed Loan drawing his revolver and without a word firing into the temple of the captive, a suspected Vietcong guerrilla, instantly killing him. Adams's photographs of the incident, which later won him the Pulitzer Prize, appeared on the front pages of newspapers throughout America and all over the world. In a conflict that had been largely depicted as being waged and suffered by indistinct participants in out-of-the-way places, the picture provided a powerful and clear close-up of the face of death in the murky chaos of war.

Eddie Adams's Pulitzer prize-winning photograph of Brigadier General Nguyen Ngoc Loan executing a suspected Vietcong guerilla on a Saigon street, February 1, 1968.

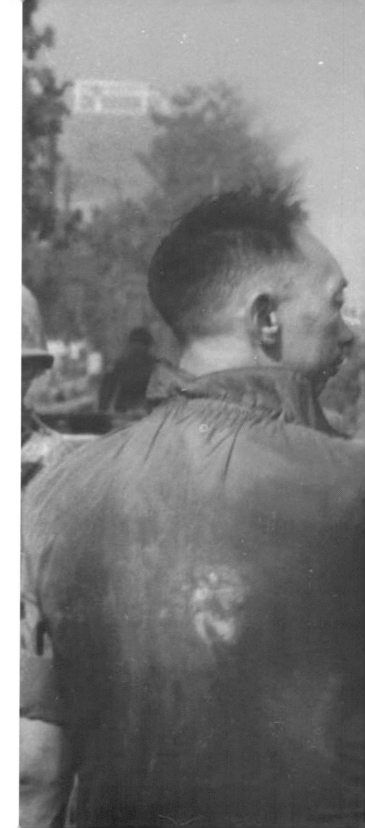

JOHNSON SAYS
HALTS NORTH
BIDS HANOI JO

ROCKEFELLER URGES ALBANY LEADERS TO SPEED BUDGET

Ready to Work With Them to Provide Funds as Fiscal Year Opens Today

By PETER KIHSS

Governor Rockefeller urged Republican and Democratic

Liberals Designate Javits; Nickerson Race Confused

Baron May Enter Race
By CLAYTON KNOWLES

The Liberal party State Committee designated Senator Jacob K. Javits for re-election late yesterday, but under conditions that confronted him with the prospect of waging a primary fight to gain the extra line on the voting machines.

A bloc of unionists in the party contending that an en-

Johnson Causes Upset

The contest for the Democratic Senate nomination in New York was thrown into confusion last night by President Johnson's announcement that he would not seek the party's nomination for re-election.

Eugene H. Nickerson, the organization's candidate for the nomination and a supporter of Senator Robert F. Kennedy,

TAX RISE PUS

Increase in War Cited—No Spe Cuts Suggest

By EILEEN SHANA
Special to The New York T

WASHINGTON, Mar
President Johnson ca
Congress tonight to "mo
debate to action, from
to voting" on a tax inc

ork Times

Temp. range: today 62-53; Sunday 68-48. Full U.S. report on Page 90.

AY, APRIL 1, 1968

10 CENTS

IE WON'T RUN;
IETNAM RAIDS;
N PEACE MOVES

MZ IS EXEMPTED

Jhnson Sets No Time imit on Halting of Air and Sea Blows

By MAX FRANKEL
Special to The New York Times

WASHINGTON, March 31— esident Johnson announced night that he had ordered a lt in the air and naval mbardment of most of North tnam and invited the Hanoi

SURPRISE DECISION

President Steps Aside in Unity Bid—Says 'House' Is Divided

Text of Johnson's address will be found on Page 26.

By TOM WICKER
Special to The New York Times

WASHINGTON, March 31— Lyndon Baines Johnson a

HOME FRONT

While the Tet Offensive raised the intensity and scale of the war in Vietnam, it also increased political divisions and cultural clashes on American soil.

President Johnson's administration and its defenders repeatedly cited the "domino theory" to explain the need to keep on fighting and commit more troops. Supporters of the war believed that the Southeast Asian countries were like a line of dominoes, ready to tumble when the first is pushed over. If Vietnam fell, they argued, it would set off a chain reaction, and one country after another would become Communist. They saw the struggle of the two Vietnams as an extension of the cold war, which meant that any North Vietnamese success signaled an unthinkable Communist victory over the United States.

Meanwhile, the war's opponents protested the government's policies of "escalation," insisting that measures such as raising the number of troops deployed and the number of bombs dropped had failed. They claimed that instead of slowing the enemy, these efforts only made the Communists more aggressive. As a result, the critics claimed, the war was turning into a "quagmire" in which America was bogged down with no clear way out.

Late in 1967, as part of a public relations campaign to convince Americans that real progress was being made in Vietnam, President Johnson had insisted that there was "a light at the end of the tunnel." In his first responses to the Tet attacks, Johnson echoed General Westmoreland's optimistic outlook. "The enemy will fail again and again," said the president at the start of February, adding, "We Americans will never yield." He rejected

Left: Women in an antiwar march, New York, April 27, 1968.

Previous page: *New York Times* front page from April 1, 1968. For full text of Johnson article, see page 116.

the views of American war critics who had been recommending a lull in the bombing as a gesture that might lead to peace talks.

But behind the tough talk, the president was stunned and shaken—both by what was happening in Vietnam and by the way the American public was reacting to those events. He was fully aware that support for his policies and his personal popularity had been steadily dwindling for some time. His anguished mood and flagging spirit could be read in his face. The once familiar image of a masterful, proud, and vain Texan who swaggered through politics like a sheriff from the Old West was gone. Increasingly the public saw an aging man with a pallid, troubled expression and sad, unsmiling eyes.

When he had come to office in 1963, Lyndon B. Johnson had been embraced by 80 percent of Americans. Bolstered by his support in the polls, he implemented his bold vision of what he termed "the Great Society." He pushed through legislation that established a nationwide preschool program called Head Start, Medicare and Medicaid, which greatly expanded medical coverage, and civil rights laws that curbed racial discrimination in housing and employment.

For a while the public had welcomed these measures. As Johnson's preoccupation with Vietnam grew, however, his favorable ratings dropped as the numbers of U.S. soldiers being killed in action rose. At the end of 1965, the average monthly death toll of Americans in Vietnam was 172; in 1967 it had risen to 779. In just the first month of 1968, 1,163 Americans had been killed, and in February, as the Tet Offensive reached a peak, the total rose to 2,197. An opinion poll taken six weeks after the Tet Offensive began showed that public support for Johnson had plummeted, with only 26 percent backing his leadership in the war.

No clear-cut national consensus on Vietnam policies emerged as winter inched toward spring in 1968. Some voices called for a rapid withdrawal of American troops, others wanted smaller, staggered reductions of troop levels, and another faction pinned its hopes on a bombing pause as a prelude to peace talks. At the same time, polls showed that many of those opposing Johnson blamed him for not being assertive enough and wanted even more bombing.

With fear and opposition to the draft rising, the attitudes and resentments of the youth movement were gaining momentum, but much of mainstream America still remained unconvinced by those who had been demanding a change in war policy. On February 27, this started to change. On that evening Walter Cronkite, the CBS news anchorman who was often called "the most trusted man in America," gave a report based on his recent trip through Vietnam. In his previous reports on the war, he had emphasized hard facts and shied away from predictions. Now his tone was startlingly different. Acknowledging that what he was about to say was "speculative, personal, subjective," he stated that he was not sure who had won and who had lost in the Tet Offensive, and declared, "We have been too often disappoint-ed by the optimism of the American leaders, both in Vietnam and Washington, to have faith any longer in the silver linings they find in the darkest clouds."

Then came his powerful ending: "To say that we are mired in stalemate seems the only realistic, yet unsatisfactory, conclusion. . . . It is increasingly clear to this reporter that the only rational way out then will be to negotiate, not as victors, but as an honorable people who

Members of the "Jeanette Rankin Brigade" (named in honor of the first woman member of Congress) in a march on Washington, January 15, 1968.

lived up to their pledge to defend democracy, and did the best they could." It was a stunning blow against Lyndon Johnson's policies.

After watching Cronkite's report, the president reportedly told an aide, "If I've lost Cronkite, I've lost middle America."

Two weeks later, another surprising development further shifted the political landscape. On March 12, the state of New Hampshire held the country's first primary election, in which registered Democrats voted for the man they wanted to nominate to run in the presidential election that November. The two names on the ballot were those of President Johnson and Eugene McCarthy. Eugene McCarthy was a senator from Minnesota who had little chance of ultimate victory in the general election. But he was hoping to use his campaign as an opportunity to draw attention to and challenge the war. That winter he had attracted teams of student volunteers who in their enthusiasm conformed to his "Clean for Gene" rules, which required them to cut their hair, shave beards, and put on ties in order to win over as many straight-laced adults as possible.

As the votes were counted, it appeared that the volunteers had done a great job. Out of 50,000 ballots cast, McCarthy received only 230 votes fewer than Johnson—the incumbent president of the United States, who less than four years earlier had won the race for the White House by the greatest margin in history.

The New Hampshire result galvanized Democratic politics. It left McCarthy thrilled and Johnson worried, but its greatest impact by far was on Robert F. Kennedy, a senator from New York who was the younger brother and had been the closest confidant of President John F. Kennedy. Bobby, as he was called, had been attorney general in JFK's cabinet, and after his brother was killed, he had quickly become the dominant figure in the Kennedy clan, the country's most powerful political family. On March 16, four days after the New Hampshire ballots were recorded, Robert F. Kennedy formally entered the race for the Democratic presidential nomination.

At that moment, the electoral stakes rose enormously. In contrast to the relatively unknown McCarthy, Bobby Kennedy would not be running to educate the nation or to make debating points. He was out to replace the sitting president.

Throughout the rest of March, the White House buzzed with consultations as matters of war and peace shaped the president's political options. It was announced that at the end of the month Johnson would make an important speech about Vietnam. As Harry McPherson, the president's speechwriter and longtime friend, began churning out drafts of that speech, Johnson sought advice from the "wise men," an elite group of senior diplomats, judges, and former generals. He also spent more and more time with Clark Clifford, a lawyer he had appointed a month earlier to take over as secre-tary of defense. In contrast to the former secre-tary, Robert McNamara, Clifford was hoping to steer Johnson toward a course of honorable withdrawal from Vietnam. As the speech was being revised, Clifford succeeded in changing the first line from "Tonight I want to talk to

Robert F. Kennedy shakes hands with supporters at a rally in California, March 24, 1968.

LYNDON B. JOHNSON

Despite the fact that the nation was frustrated and angry about the war in Vietnam, troubled by racial strife, and caught up in inflation, most Americans had more or less assumed that Johnson, the highly political and mightily proud thirty-sixth president of the United States, would run for reelection in 1968.

But in his televised speech, Johnson first gave the long-awaited word that he had ordered a major reduction in the bombing of Communist North Vietnam and called for peace talks.

Then he said he would not be a candidate for another term.

With those electrifying words, Johnson admitted the shattering of a dream he had cherished since November 22, 1963, when a madman's bullet killed his predecessor and made him president: that he would restore peace and serenity to the American people.

He set forth those goals in a ringing speech before a joint session of Congress on March 15, 1965.

I want to be the president who educated young children to the wonders of their world.

I want to be the president who helped to feed the hungry and to prepare them to be taxpayers instead of tax-eaters.

I want to be the president who helped the poor find their own way and who protected the right of every citizen to vote in every election.

I want to be the president who helped to end the hatred among his fellow men and who promoted love among the people of all races, all regions, and all parties.

I want to be the president who helped to end war among the brothers of this earth.

These were Lyndon Johnson's aims, but few of them were to be achieved. Less than two years after that fateful day in Dallas when John F. Kennedy was shot, and less than a year after he had been chosen president in his own right, President Johnson found himself trapped in a remote, bloody, and incredibly costly war that, it seemed, would never end.

Johnson's 1,500-word inaugural address was one of the shortest in history. In it he said: *"In a land of great wealth, families must not live in hopeless poverty. In a land rich in harvest, children must not go hungry. In a land of healing miracles, neighbors must not suffer and die untended. In a great land of learning and scholars, young people must be taught to read and write."*

The president had good reason to believe that many of his dreams for a better America could become reality, for the voters, while putting him into office in a landslide, had given him a Congress dominated by Democrats.

What the president called "the fabulous eighty-ninth Congress" soon began to enact far-reaching programs. One of the measures that would have the most far-reaching effect was the Medicare bill, which provided virtually free medical and hospital care for the aged under Social Security.

Johnson's view of what he achieved might be summed up in a homily he once delivered to a group of young people.

"To hunger for use and to go unused is the worst hunger of all," he said. "Few men have the power by a single act or by a single lifetime to shape history for themselves. Presidents, for example, quickly realize that while a single act might destroy the world they live in, no one single decision can make life suddenly better or can turn history around for the good."

you about the war in Vietnam" to "Tonight I want to speak to you of peace in Vietnam and Southeast Asia."

But it was the very last segment of the speech that turned out to be the most dramatic. On March 30, a day before the speech was to be given, Johnson met with McPherson and Clifford to review the final draft. At one point McPherson apologized for not yet having prepared the final section. Johnson turned to him and said, "Don't worry, I may have a little ending of my own."

Even the president's top advisers did not learn what he had in mind until just a few hours before Johnson faced the cameras at nine o'clock. As for the rest of the White House staff, they learned of Johnson's staggering decision only when, with the rest of the American public, they heard him announce it at the end of his address. I was working that Sunday night and was clustered with several coworkers around one of the TV screens in the newsroom. When I heard Johnson reverse his earlier position to announce he was ordering a halt in the bombing, I assumed that this would be the main point of the speech.

Then, after an extended review of American foreign policy, Johnson shifted into his surprising summation: "With American sons in the fields far away, with America's future under challenge right here at home, with our hopes and the world's hopes for peace in the balance every day, I do not believe I should devote an hour or a day of my time to any personal partisan causes or to any duties other than the awesome duties of this office—the presidency of your country." Talking slowly but firmly, he added: "Accordingly, I shall not seek, and I will not accept, the nomination of my party for another term as your president."

There were gasps in the newsroom. It was the first time that I ever heard the senior editor on duty give the command so often seen in the movies. "Stop the presses," shouted Larry Hauck, ordering the pressroom to interrupt its run until a new story and headline could be prepared to take account of Johnson's declaration.

"All the News That's Fit to Print"

The New York T[...]

VOL. CXVII . No. 40,249

© 1968 The New York Times Company.

NEW YORK, [...]

MARTIN LUTHER KING[...]
A WHITE IS SUSPECTE[...]

JOHNSON DELAYS TRIP TO HAWAII; MAY LEAVE TODAY

President Spends a Hectic Day Here and in Capital —Sees Thant at the U.N.

By MAX FRANKEL
Special to The New York Times

WASHINGTON, April 4 — President Johnson postponed his trip to Hawaii at least until tomorrow after he heard of the death of the Rev. Dr. Martin Luther King Jr. tonight.

The news, which visibly shocked the President, came at the end of one of the most ex-

Hanoi Charges U.S. Raid Far North of 20th Parallel

By EVERT CLARK
Special to The New York Times

WASHINGTON, April 4 — North Vietnam charged in a broadcast today that United States planes had bombed a "populated area" in northwestern Vietnam far north of the 20th parallel. The Defense Department said it knew of no such raid but was investigating.

President Johnson has ordered that there be no attacks on North Vietnam north of the 20th Parallel as a step toward de-escalating the war.

[In South Vietnam, United States marines beat off an attack by about 400 North Vietnamese soldiers charging up a hill near Khesanh, kill-

DISMAY IN NATI[...]

Negroes Urge Oth[...] to Carry on Spi[...] of Nonviolence[...]

By LAWRENCE VAN G[...]

Dismay, shame, ange[...] foreboding marked the n[...] reaction last night to th[...] Dr. Martin Luther Kin[...] murder.

From the high offices [...] to the man in the street[...] of the moderate civil [...] leader's violent death in [...] phis yesterday drew, f[...] most part, stunned and [...] statements.

Most major Negro or[...] tions and Negro lead[...]

rk Times

Weather: Clearing today.
cold tonight. Fair, cool tomorrow.
Temp. range: today 62-44; Thurs.
73-52. Full U.S. report on Page 92.

10 CENTS

, APRIL 5, 1968

S SLAIN IN MEMPHIS;
JOHNSON URGES CALM

ESIDENT'S PLEA

TV, He Deplores Brutal' Murder of Negro Leader

atements by Johnson and
Humphrey are on Page 24.

Special to The New York Times

WASHINGTON, April 4—
esident Johnson deplored to-
ght in a brief television ad-
ess to the nation the "brutal
ying" of the Rev. Dr. Martin
ther King Jr.

He asked "every citizen to re-
ct the blind violence that has
ruck Dr. King, who lived by
nviolence."

Mr. Johnson said he was

GUARD CALLED OUT

Curfew Is Ordered in Memphis, but Fires and Looting Erupt

By EARL CALDWELL
Special to The New York Times

MEMPHIS, Friday, April 5—
The Rev. Dr. Martin Luth
King Jr., who preached no
violence and racial brothe
hood, was fatally shot here la
night by a distant gunman w
then raced away and escape

Four thousand Natio
Guard troops were ordered i
Memphis by Gov. Buford
lington after the 39-year-
Nobel Prize-winning civil rig
leader died.

A curfew was imposed
the shocked city of 550,000

MARTIN LUTHER KING, JR.

On the evening of Friday, April 4, just four days after President Johnson's announcement, the Reverand Dr. Martin Luther King, Jr., was shot and killed. The thirty-nine-year-old preacher, whose nonviolent campaigns had exposed and chipped away at practices that denied equality, justice, and opportunity to millions of black Americans, was silenced by a single rifle shot that broke his spine as he leaned over a balcony railing at the Lorraine Motel in Memphis, Tennessee. He was in Memphis to support a long strike of black sanitation workers, and just before the fatal shot, he had asked a musician friend to sing a spiritual at a strike rally that King was to address later that evening.

The news of King's violent death staggered the nation, even more profoundly and certainly more visibly than Johnson's abdication. Serious rioting, largely by black youths, broke out in a number of cities, among them Chicago, Boston, Detroit, Raleigh, Tallahassee, and Memphis. Washington, the nation's capital, was the hardest hit, with eruptions of looting and arson that at one point drew to within a few blocks of the White House. Through the troubled days and nights, more than 15,000 federal troops and National Guardsmen patrolled the city's streets.

President Johnson declared a national day of mourning, and King was buried in Atlanta with an enormous funeral procession in which tens of thousands marched and sang "We Shall Overcome," an anthem of the civil rights movement. But violence continued to flare in Hartford, Pittsburgh, Newark, and Baltimore.

While national figures, politicians, athletes,

Left: A mule-drawn wagon carrying the casket of Dr. Martin Luther King, Jr., through the streets of Atlanta, followed by dignitaries and thousands of mourners, April 9, 1968.

Previous page: *New York Times* front page from April 5, 1968. For full text of Martin Luther King, Jr., article, see page 119.

union officials, and show business stars joined black civil rights leaders in praising King and evoking his dream of racial harmony, others urged that greater force be used to crush the riots. Chicago's mayor, Richard Daley, instructed his police to "shoot to kill arsonists" and to "shoot to maim or cripple looters." Meanwhile, younger and more militant black leaders such as Stokely Carmichael and H. Rap Brown, who had rejected King's reliance on nonviolence in favor of "black power," now urged infuriated blacks to arm themselves for confrontational struggle.

When after two weeks the violence finally subsided, thirty-nine people had been killed, all but five of them black. Nearly 20,000 people had been arrested in riots that had raged in 130 cities. Throughout the country, close to 65,000 troops had been deployed in riot duty to reinforce local and state police.

The death of Martin Luther King, Jr., had come just five weeks after a special presidential advisory panel released the Kerner Report, a detailed assessment of race relations in the United States. The advisory panel had spent a year studying the implications of the rioting that had occurred in several northern cities the summer before, and had presented in its report

A soldier stands guard on a Washington, D.C., street following a night of arson and looting in response to the assassination of Martin Luther King, Jr., April 5, 1968.

this dire forecast: "Our nation is moving toward two societies, one black, one white—separate and unequal." The eleven-member National Advisory Commission on Civil Disorders, headed by Governor Otto Kerner of Illinois, concluded that "white racism" had been chiefly to blame for the explosive conditions that triggered the summer riots of 1967.

The panel identified the primary causes of the riots to be the common frustrations of ghetto dwellers over "pervasive discrimination and segregation in employment, education, and housing." They also cited the widespread belief of many young blacks that police routinely treated black people with greater and more frequent brutality than they employed in their dealings with whites. In its recommendations, the panel urged sweeping reform in law enforcement, welfare, employment, and education at national and local levels. It also criticized the way black communities were covered by private media outlets with predominantly white staffs. While the report did not offer any particular legislation or specify the costs of such a comprehensive approach, it warned that if drastic and expansive measures were not undertaken immediately, it would be very hard to impede the "continuing polarization of

the American community and ultimately, the destruction of basic democratic values."

When the Kerner Commission had issued its report on February 29, it had been front-page news in many newspapers. *The New York Times* even printed its full 4,000-word summary. But with the consequences of the Tet Offensive still playing out in Vietnam and reverberating in Washington, discussion of the Kerner Report soon subsided. Then suddenly King's murder and the renewed wave of ghetto violence brought the commission's findings into sharp focus, as its dismal projections of a racially divided America were reinforced by daily events.

As the FBI mounted an international search for King's suspected shooter, a man identified as a segregationist named James Earl Ray, it was generally understood that King had been killed because of his teachings and actions. King had spent his whole working life in non-violent struggle against segregation and discriminatory divisions of society and humanity. He transformed the historic struggle for black equality into an effective modern civil rights movement.

Over the years, King's house had been bombed, shots had been fired at his door, and

A Memphis police officer swings his nightstick at a suspected looter during rioting that erupted during a civil rights march, Memphis, March 28, 1968.

he was jailed, ridiculed, stabbed, and punched. Meanwhile, J. Edgar Hoover, the politically manipulative director of the FBI, ordered his agents to spy on King's private life, looking for information that might be used to pressure or intimidate him.

Minutes after King was shot, I was assigned to spend the night in Harlem, where, in case of rioting, the police were quickly establishing a command post in a small park off 125th Street. As things turned out, there was nothing for me to report, as Harlem, though angry and tense, remained calm.

I sat on a bench looking out over parked police cars at the quiet streets of the country's most famous black community and recalled the only time I had seen and heard Martin Luther King, Jr. It happened to have been when he made his greatest and most quoted speech, the one in which he declared, "I have a dream." Along with a *Times* colleague, Paul Montgomery, I had attended the mammoth March on Washington on April 28, 1963. Arriving at dawn, we had watched as the city filled up. Cars and buses with southern license plates dropped off groups of black people, most of them wearing their Sunday best. Gradually the crowd had thickened and moved toward the lawn stretching from the

Martin Luther King, Jr., addresses the crowd gathered at the Lincoln Memorial for the March on Washington, August 28, 1963.

MARTIN LUTHER KING, JR.

To millions of black Americans, the Rev. Dr. Martin Luther King, Jr., was the prophet of their crusade for racial equality. He was their voice of anguish, their eloquence in humiliation, their battle cry for human dignity. He forged for them the weapons of nonviolence that withstood and blunted the ferocity of segregation.

And to many millions of white Americans, he was one of a group of blacks who preserved the bridge of communication between races when racial warfare threatened the United States in the sixties, as African Americans sought the full emancipation pledged to them a century before by Abraham Lincoln.

To the world, Dr. King had the stature of a winner of the Nobel Peace Prize—a man with access to the White House and the Vatican, a hero in the African states that were just emerging from colonialism.

Inevitably, as a symbol of integration, he became the object of unrelenting attacks and vilification. Threats became so commonplace that his wife, Coretta, could ignore burning crosses on the lawn and ominous phone calls. Through it all he adhered to a creed of passive disobedience that infuriated segregationists.

Dr. King's belief in nonviolence was subjected to intense pressure in 1966, when some black groups adopted the slogan "black power" in the aftermath of civil rights marches into Mississippi and race riots in northern cities. He rejected the idea, saying:

"The Negro needs the white man to free him from his fears. The white man needs the Negro to free him from his guilt. A doctrine of black supremacy is as evil as a doctrine of white supremacy."

Dr. King had a way of reducing complex issues to terms that anyone could understand. In the summer of 1965, when there was widespread discontent among blacks about their struggle for equality of employment, he declared, "What good does it do to be able to eat at a lunch counter if you can't buy a hamburger?"

The enormous impact of Dr. King's words was one of the reasons he was in the President's Room in the Capitol on August 6, 1965, when President Johnson signed the Voting Rights Act, which struck down literacy tests, provided federal registrars to assure the ballot to unregistered blacks, and marked the growth of African Americans as a political force in the South.

There was no false modesty in Dr. King's self-appraisal of his role in the civil rights movement.

"History," he said, "has thrust me into this position. It would be both immoral and a sign of ingratitude if I did not face my moral responsibility to do what I can in this struggle."

Lincoln Memorial. We came upon a young white guitarist who was singing a song that included the line "The times, they are a-changing." Paul found out the singer's name and called in the information for possible use. The result was a paragraph in the next day's coverage, which Paul claims was the *Times*'s first-ever mention of Bob Dylan (except that his name was misspelled as Dillon).

Eventually the crowd had grown to 250,000 people, making it the largest gathering that had ever taken place in Washington. While blacks dominated, whites could easily be spotted in every part of the crowd. Labor leaders spoke; so did politicians, actors, writers, ministers, priests, and rabbis. Then, toward the end of the program, Martin Luther King, Jr., delivered the relatively short speech that has been compared to Abraham Lincoln's magnificent Gettysburg Address for its eloquence and poetic imagery. I recall King's rolling cadences as he shared his inspirational dream with the crowd and his country:

I have a dream that one day this nation will rise up and live out the true meaning of its creed: "We hold these truths to be self-evident; that all men are created equal."

I have a dream that one day on the red hills of Georgia the sons of former slaves and the sons of former slave owners will be able to sit down together at the table of brotherhood.

I have a dream that one day even the state of Mississippi, a state sweltering with the heat of injustice, sweltering with the heat of oppression, will be transformed into an oasis of freedom and justice.

I have a dream that my four little children will one day live in a nation where they will not be judged by the color of their skin but by the content of their character.

I have a dream today.

I have a dream that one day down in Alabama, with its vicious racists, with its governor having his lips dripping with the words of interposition and nullification, that one day right down in Alabama little black boys and black girls will be able to join hands with little white boys and white girls as sisters and brothers.

I have a dream today.

Five years later, as I sat through the night in Harlem, I wondered like so many other Americans whether that dream would remain alive now that the man who had dreamed it and promoted it so passionately was gone.

increase in its ...
rate, the discount rate, which
was intended to slow the pres-

Continued on Page 28, Column 3

26 HOUSING UNITS FACE RISE IN RENT

City Asked to Grant Added Tax Relief to 12 Projects

The Lindsay administration said yesterday that it was raising rents or carrying charges in 26 middle-income housing projects throughout the city. Most of the increases will come to 15 per cent, bringing the average rents to about $35 a room.

The increases were disclosed in a letter to the Board of Estimate from Jason R. Nathan, Administrator of Housing and Development, who asked the board to grant increased tax relief for 12 of the projects that face particularly severe financial pressures.

About 1,500 of the more than 10,000 persons residing in the developments that face rent increases picketed City Hall and met with John McGarrahan, an assistant to Mayor Lindsay.

Tenants in a number of rental and cooperative middle-income projects have vowed to withhold rents to protest the rising cost of middle-income housing.

Mr. Nathan said that the increased rents and carrying charges were ordered only after an "exhaustive" review of the

Continued on Page 56, Column 1

Rioting in Summer

An Army study group, under the direction of Brig. Gen. John J. Hennessey, deputy director of Army operations, is studying other lessons learned during the lootings and rioting that erupted in a number of cities after Dr. King's slaying in Memphis on April 4, the sources said.

Before Dr. King's assassination, the Army had designated seven brigade-level task forces of about 2,000 men each for riot control duty. This was one of a number of preparations for this summer made as a result of planning that followed the major riots in Newark and De-

Continued on Page 30, Column 6

U.S. Catholic Bishops Endorse Riot Report

By EDWARD B. FISKE
Special to The New York Times

ST. LOUIS, April 23—The American bishops of the Roman Catholic Church today endorsed the conclusion of the National Advisory Commission on Civil Disorders that white racism was the major cause of racial turmoil in the nation's cities.

In a seven-page report adopted this morning, the members of the National Conference of Catholic Bishops called for large programs in the dioceses to combat racial injustice. They urged that the programs be carried out in full cooperation with Protestants and Jews.

The 250 bishops opened their annual spring meeting today at the Chase-Park Plaza Hotel under conditions of strict secrecy.

$100,000 from the Robert R. McCormick Charitable Trust,

Continued on Page 31, Column 2

required for passage on ...
message. Because the ori...

Continued on Page 30, Colu...

300 Protesting Columbia Studen...

Columbia students sitting in Hamilton Hall yester...

By DAVID BIRD

Three - hundred chanting students barricaded the Dean of Columbia College in his office yesterday to protest the construction of a gymnasium in Morningside Park and a defense-oriented program

against the gymnasium tended at one time to building site, where stu... tore down a section of before being driven off policemen. The student that construction of the nasium would be "racis...

by China's position at the
for discussion at the
ued on Page 18, Column 3
for its target, and the United
Continued on Page 11, Column 1

rricade Office of College Dean

The New York Times (by Neal Boenzi)

ed to speakers protest against university's policies

nal facilities. The charge inst the defense program.

Institute for Defense alysis, was that it sup rted the war effort in Viet m. The protest, organized the leftist Students for a mocratic Society, had the

tives of several Negro organi zations unrelated to Columbia joined the protest. Among the groups were the Harlem chapter of the Congress of Racial Equality, the Harlem Committee for Self-Defense, the United Black Front, and

to encounter objections from many of the nonnuclear states.

Unless there is an overwhelming Assembly vote to postpone signature of the treaty, as some nonnuclear states are expected to propose, the American and Soviet intention is to open the treaty to signature and ratification once the debate is concluded.

There will still remain the problem, however, of obtaining the signatures of such nations, as India, Israel, West Germany and Brazil, which have been critical of the draft. It is in this connection that the threat to cut off assistance in the

Continued on Page 9, Column 1

Strikers Support Tory's Race Views

By ANTHONY LEWIS
Special to The New York Times

LONDON, April 23—More than 2,000 London dockers quit work today to demonstrate support for Enoch Powell's view that Britain has too many colored immigrants.

Hundreds of the dockers marched on Westminster. They mobbed the central parliamentary lobby and cheered right-wing backers of Mr. Powell, who was ousted from the Conservative leadership Sunday for a speech the Tory leader, Edward Heath, termed racist.

In the House of Commons, both Labor and Conservative spokesmen pleaded for calm on the racial issue that has exploded here. Before the House was the Government's race relations bill, which would pro-

the French would be pleased
Continued on Page 13, Column 1

TRUDEAU ORDERS JUNE 25 ELECTION

New Canadian Chief Seeks a Clear Liberal Majority

By JAY WALZ
Special to The New York Times

OTTAWA, April 23—Pierre Elliott Trudeau met Parliament for the first time as Prime Minister this afternoon and immediately dissolved it to call a general election for June 25.

Mr. Trudeau's call, made just three days after his induction as Canada's 15th Prime Minister, was a bold effort to win a majority for the Liberals. A majority government would be Canada's first since 1962. There have been four elections in the last 10 years. The last three resulted in minority governments.

Influential party advisers prevailed upon Mr. Trudeau to act quickly in an effort to reverse the pattern. They argued that he should seek to capitalize on the popular enthusiasm and

Continued on Page 15, Column 1

NEWS INDEX

COLUMBIA UNIVERSITY

Five days after Dr. King's death, at a memorial service being held for him at Columbia University, a twenty-year-old campus radical named Mark Rudd mounted the stage and seized the microphone. He angrily denounced the school's president, Grayson Kirk, for committing what he called "a moral outrage against the memory of Dr. King."

Rudd, the president of the Columbia University chapter of a student organization called Students for a Democratic Society (SDS), was trying to intensify an ongoing campaign to portray the university as racist for its treatment of a neighboring black community. At the same time, he was lashing out at the school administration for supporting the government's war efforts in Vietnam.

The group's earlier attempts to stir protest had not been very effective. Just six months earlier, Columbia students had disregarded SDS urgings and voted overwhelmingly to allow all government agencies, including the armed services, to come onto the campus to recruit students for possible employment. But as so often happened in 1968, opinions and emotions shifted dramatically and suddenly. In his remarks at the King memorial, Rudd made a vital connection. He linked issues of race with anger over the Vietnam War while engaging the passions, idealism, and energy of the audience.

Rudd specifically targeted a Columbia University project to build a gymnasium in a Harlem park just south of the school's campus. The university, he charged, was "steal[ing] land from the people of Harlem." Then, after school officials unplugged the microphone, he accused them of hypocrisy, shouting that while

Left: New York police move in on demonstrating students, putting an end to the protests at Columbia University, April 30, 1968.

Previous page: *New York Times* front page from April 24, 1968. For full text of Columbia University article, see page 123.

they praised Dr. King for civil disobedience, they suppressed campus dissent.

Over the next few days, confrontation mounted. Dr. Kirk banned all indoor demonstrations. Then Rudd led a protest of 150 students, carrying a petition insisting that Columbia break its ties with an organization, called the Institute for Defense Analysis (IDA), which examined and advised the government on military strategy. The university suspended Rudd and five other SDS members. Students who continued to demand an end to the gym construction now also chanted, "Free the IDA six," in reference to those suspended. Rudd published an open letter to Kirk in which he referred to Kirk's use of the term "generation gap" to describe the growing gulf between the young and their elders. Rudd explained how he interpreted the meaning of the phrase. "I see it as a real conflict between those who run things now—you Grayson Kirk—and those who feel oppressed by and disgusted with the society you rule—the young people."

On Tuesday, April 23, several hundred students gathered at the center of campus to hear Rudd deliver another speech. At one point, as a group of student athletes recognizable as "jocks" by their ties, sport jackets, and short hair stood off to one side shouting support for Kirk and glowering, Rudd and Ted Gold, the SDS vice president, asked the crowd what

should be done. Someone shouted "to Low," referring to the domed Low Library, where Dr. Kirk had his offices. When the crowd reached the building, they found the doors locked. Then someone else shouted, "Tear down the fence," meaning the fence around the site for the proposed gym, and again the crowd, by then numbering around five hundred, ran the four blocks into the park, where they failed to batter down the fence.

Another voice shouted, "Seize Hamilton Hall!" and this time the group surged to an academic building, barricading a dean in his office and settling into the classrooms and corridors, where they would remain locked in for the next seven days.

Along with about a half dozen other *Times* reporters, I spent most of the next week on the Columbia campus, first in Hamilton Hall and then in four other buildings that were later occupied. As hundreds of students swarmed into the buildings, discussions of politics, world affairs, and culture rang out everywhere, ranging beyond the gym and the war. Often the name of Frantz Fannon, a black psychoanalyst from Martinique, came up. Before his death in 1961, Fannon had written about how the legacy of colonialism continued to shape patterns of racism and oppression. Another figure often mentioned was Herbert Marcuse, a social philosopher who had fled Nazi Germany.

Marcuse taught at American universities and described how the expansion of democracy was being curbed both in Communist societies and under contemporary capitalism. His backers enthusiastically talked of encouraging "participatory democracy" while scorning the "oppressive tolerance" that, according to Marcuse, led American newspapers, radio, and TV stations to become timid copies of one another rather than providing a variety of viewpoints and policy choices.

Posters went up with portraits of China's Mao Tse Tung, Cuba's Fidel Castro, and Che Guevara, the Latin American revolutionary. There were also images of generational heroes, among them singers such as Bob Dylan, Janis Joplin, The Beatles, and Aretha Franklin. Some students proclaimed their admiration for three

Mark Rudd is interviewed by the media outside the Low Library, April 25, 1968, two days after taking control of the building.

earlier Columbia students—Alan Ginsburg, Jack Kerouac, and William Burroughs—who had established the "Beat Generation" through their writings about spontaneous ramblings and sensory experimentation. There were also iconic images of marijuana plants and of the Zig-Zag man, the logo of a popular brand of cigarette papers.

Within two days, more than 1,000 students, along with some of their off-campus allies, were camping out in the classrooms and hallways, clustering with friends and ideological soul mates. Banners were hung to mark off distinct "liberated zones." Red armbands identified people who were ready for a "real" revolution, while those wearing green armbands signaled their support for the strike as long as it remained nonviolent.

As the student strike attracted greater television and newspaper coverage, its impact in

Students protest outside the Cathedral of St. John the Divine during Columbia University commencement, June 4, 1968.

and beyond New York City grew. There had been campus sit-ins at other schools, usually limited demonstrations taking place at remote college towns. Columbia was one of the country's most prestigious universities, an elite Ivy League school in the heart of the country's largest city and its media capital. At that time, commentators would often use the term "the establishment" to describe the layer of society that ran America's most important institutions. Clearly Columbia, and the privileged students who studied there, were part of "the establishment."

Suddenly, in full view of television cameras, Columbia students could be seen enthusiastically turning their backs on the establishment, mocking its representatives in often vulgar and obscene language. Female students taunted policemen by calling them "pigs." Such behavior mystified many of the students' elders, some of whom wrote letters to newspapers asking, *Who are these young people? What has changed them from well-behaved middle-class achievers into would-be revolutionaries and nonconformists? Is it drugs? Is it the music? Is it newly available birth control devices and permissive attitudes about sex? Is it the war in Vietnam, the draft, the civil rights movement, the killing of Dr. King? Or, is it all of the above?*

There were numerous explanations. Some noted that this new, assertive "youth culture"

appeared as the earliest baby boomers—members of the unusually large generation that was born during the population surge following World War II—became young adults. Sociologists suggested that these boomers commanded more attention precisely because of their numbers. Seeking to increase sales and profits, clothing manufacturers, record companies, moviemakers, and publishers increasingly catered to the tastes and wishes of this age group, and its members grew increasingly aware of their rising power.

While some of the Columbia protesters hoped to steer the campus furor toward their

Black power militants Stokely Carmichael (left) and H. Rap Brown leave Hamilton Hall, which black students occupied, April 26, 1968.

own political goals, the general mood at the outset of the strike was more festive than militant. Some professors crossed into the occupied buildings to join in the discussions. Soon after Fayerweather Hall was seized on Wednesday, April 25, a call went out over a bullhorn "for girls to volunteer to cook." A young woman stood up and shouted, "Liberated women do not cook, they are not cooks." There was laugh-

ter, and then some young men, along with some women, went off to prepare heaps of spaghetti. At one point a dating couple decided to get married, and one of the university chaplains came to conduct the ceremony.

As the weekend approached, each of the occupied buildings was developing its own character. Early on, the strike committee had divided along racial lines after black students

Demonsrators injured in clashes with police are treated at an emergency infirmary, April 29, 1968.

and their neighborhood allies from Harlem asked the SDS faction to leave Hamilton Hall. The whites left and set up headquarters in Dr. Kirk's office in the Low Library, where Tom Hayden, the twenty-seven-year-old leader of the national SDS movement, held conferences and gave interviews.

Fayerweather, where green armbands outnumbered red ones, had almost constant teach-ins. Avery, the home of the architecture school, had no barricades and people could walk in and out freely. A design-in had been organized to consider what kind of gym could serve both the school and the neighborhood.

Police massed outside the campus, and the student-run radio station kept reporting on their movements. Talks were held between Dr. Kirk, the police, and the city's mayor, John Lindsay. By late Monday night on April 29, my *Times* colleagues and I took up positions in various parts of the campus, waiting for what our editors told us could be an imminent police assault. The "bust" began at two-thirty Tuesday morning, when 1,000 policemen stormed onto the campus with their nightsticks drawn. From my perch near Avery Hall, I heard students shout insults but saw no real resistance. But many students were beaten, kicked, and punched. Girls were pulled by the hair, faculty members were beaten by the police, and so too were some of the jocks who

had come out to cheer the uniformed raiders. At one point I found my *Times* colleague and friend, Robert McG. Thomas, a burly six-foot-five-inch reporter, with blood streaming from a head wound caused by a police baton.

By dawn, 148 people were taken to emergency rooms with injuries and 720 students had been arrested. Later, 120 charges of police brutality were filed.

The consequences of the occupation and the assault were varied. Rudd remained suspended but vowed to continue the strike. Ted Gold would later join a radical group called the Weather Underground. On March 6, 1970, he and two of his colleagues were killed in a Greenwich Village townhouse when a bomb, which one of Gold's housemates was preparing to plant at a New Jersey army base, exploded. As for the Columbia president, Grayson Kirk—within three months he resigned.

The raid and images of police brutality left a powerful impression in the minds of the public, shocking even many of those who had disapproved of the student takeover. Work on the gymnasium was suspended.

For years to come, the events at Columbia would serve to mobilize young people at other campuses. Tom Hayden later wrote that the nationwide goal had been declared by a slogan scrawled on one of the university buildings. It said, "Create two, three, many Columbias."

"All the News That's Fit to Print"

The New York

VOL. CXVII. No. 40,299   © 1968 The New York Times Company.   NEW YORK, SA

NEW SCHOOL PLAN PUTS ALBANY NEAR '68 ADJOURNMENT

Compromise Calls for Mild Decentralization Program Acceptable to Union

BILLS PASSED IN A RUSH

$290-Million Approved for Cities, Adding $100-Million More Here Next Year

By SYDNEY H. SCHANBERG
Special to The New York Times

ALBANY, Saturday, May 25 —The 1968 Legislature stumbled toward adjournment today after removing the last major obstacle—resolution of the racially sensitive controversy over decentralization of the New York City school system.

The Senate passed early this morning, and the Assembly was expected to follow suit later in the day, a mild decentralization plan that was agreed to late last

Goldwater Awarded $75,000 in Damages In His Suit for Libel

By EDWARD C. BURKS

Barry Goldwater was awarded $75,000 in "punitive damages" by a Federal Court jury here early this morning in his libel suit against Ralph Ginzburg, the publisher, and Fact magazine.

A jury of nine men and three women decided that the 1964 Republican Presidential candidate had been subjected to deliberate character assassination in the October, 1964, issue of Fact, devoted to "The Mind of Barry Goldwater." The issue sold 160,000 copies.

The jury deliberated since 10:50 A.M. before Gustave H. Danitz, its foreman, read aloud the verdict and announced the award of punitive damages in a clear voice in the high-ceilinged, paneled

Continued on Page 22, Column 3

BANK HERE RAISES BORROWING COSTS

HANOI SCORES U.S. AS BEING EVASIVE ON BOMBING HALT

Foe Also Says Americans Intensify Ground War— Accusations Are Denied

By HEDRICK SMITH
Special to The New York Times

PARIS, May 24—A North Vietnamese spokesman here accused the United States negotiators today of dodging Hanoi's demand for a cessation of the bombing of the North. At the same time, he charged that American forces in the field were intensifying the war.

Both charges were rejected by an American spokesman at a press briefing. For the first time, representatives of the North Vietnamese press agency attended the briefing.

The exchanges took place indirectly through news conferences during a four-day recess in the official conversations. The next session between United States and North Vietnamese negotiating teams will be held

DE GA PROM ASKS

rk Times

LATE CITY EDITION

Weather: Mostly sunny, cool today;
fair tonight. Sunny, cool tomorrow.
Temp. range: today 65-48; Friday
61-52. Full U.S. report on Page 70.

AY, MAY 25, 1968

10 CENTS

LLE SETS A REFERENDUM;
ES TO RESIGN IF HE LOSES;
LM, BUT FIGHTING FLARES

REFORM PLANNED

Voters Will Consider University Changes, Economic Steps

Text of the de Gaulle speech is printed on Page 14.

By HENRY TANNER
Special to The New York Times

PARIS, Saturday May 25—
President de Gaulle asked the
French people last night to give
him a personal vote of confidence and said he would resign
if he did not get it.

In a seven-minute televised
address, the President announced that the Government

PARIS

American students weren't alone in their desire to be heard. An ocean away, demonstrations had been breaking out in France. Less than a week after the Columbia University protests came to an end, the unrest in France grew into a wide-scale conflict that made the turmoil at Columbia look like child's play.

There were similarities between the events in Paris and those in New York. Both were triggered by relatively minor issues, and both escalated once adult authorities singled out particular students for punishment. Underlying both upheavals was the resentment felt by young people who were frustrated that their voices and opinions were not being heard. But while the confrontation at Columbia had been largely confined to the campus, the spark ignited by students in Paris set off a windswept wildfire that quickly engulfed all of French soci-ety and threatened to bring down the government of France.

The roots of the trouble dated back to the previous winter, when a group of students at the University of Nanterre, a division of the University of Paris on the outskirts of the city, demanded a change in the rules that would keep male students from ever visiting women students in their dorms, while allowing only women who were twenty-one or older or who had the written consent of their parents to visit men in their rooms.

As discussions were held between the faculty and students, a few dozen activists emerged, calling themselves *les enragés*, meaning "the angry ones." Their leader was Daniel Cohn-Bendit, a twenty-two-year-old student with bright red hair and a wide, captivating smile.

Left: Rioting students throw stones at police, May 7, 1968.

Previous page: *New York Times* front page from May 25, 1968. For full text of Paris article, see page 126.

CHARLES DE GAULLE

Charles de Gaulle appeared tailored to the role of a man of destiny. In 1940, after the invasion of France by Germany, he rose to international attention by sending out a radio broadcast from Great Britain, encouraging his countrymen to fight on.

"For remember this," he said, "France is not alone. She is not alone. She is not alone. . . . whatever happens, the flame of French resistance must not and shall not die."

He strode into the pantheon of heroes in August, 1944, as he led a Paris liberation parade from the Arch of Triumph to Notre Dame. Cheered by two million people in an explosion of national fervor, he experienced his finest hour.

As president of France, De Gaulle's European policy was aimed at restoring France to a position of greatness. This involved, on the one hand, an informal alliance with the Soviet Union and, on the other, an effort to keep Britain and the United States at a distance.

De Gaulle's first term as President expired in January, 1966. He was elected to a second term, but only after a runoff in which he received 55 per cent of the votes.

It was domestic discontent that eventually brought him down. His conservative domestic policies cost millions of francs, which meant austerity at home at a time when a nation of chiefly small shopkeepers and farmers was struggling to transform itself into a more modern country. Inflation and wage restraints bore heavily on the working class.

In education, more students than ever before crowded the universities and studied under curriculums that were clearly irrelevant to the times. In an effort to accommodate the influx of students, satellites of older universities were set up, as at Nanterre, just outside Paris.

Following the May events of 1968, de Gaulle won a big victory in the elections by posing a choice between chaos and himself. He seemed more in control than ever. However, as Georges Pompidou, then the Premier, remarked shortly after the student-worker insurgency, "Things would never be quite the same again."

The proof that de Gaulle had lost the adherence of his people came over a relatively minor issue that was to be settled in a referendum and which at first created only slight interest.

Then de Gaulle injected himself. He declared that the vote was to be a test of public confidence. "Your reply is going to determine the destiny of France," he told the French people on April 25, 1969, "because if I am disavowed by the majority of you, my present task as chief of state would obviously become impossible [and] I would immediately stop exercising my functions."

Two days after his appeal for confidence Charles de Gaulle was repudiated by 53 percent of the voters. And within 12 hours he departed the splendorous Elysée Palace on the banks of the Seine in Paris, his residence for almost 11 years, for his plain home in the tiny village of Colombey-les-Deux-Eglises. More than the end of a singular political reign, it was the end of an era.

A proponent of what was being termed "the New Left," Cohn-Bendit was suspicious of both sides in the cold war. Along with the other angry ones, he moved beyond restrictive visiting rules to denounce other aspects of French higher education—such as overcrowded schools and autocratic teachers who limited open discussion.

On March 22, 1968, after weeks of agitation at Nanterre that went largely unnoticed by most of France, Cohn-Bendit led five hundred supporters to seize a faculty lounge and occupy it overnight. On May 2 he received an order to appear four days later before a University of Paris disciplinary board.

The Nanterre students responded to the summons with yet another protest, which led the Ministry of Education to shut down the school. The students left their out-of-the-way suburban campus and flocked to the world-famous Sorbonne in the heart of Paris. There, Cohn-Bendit found a megaphone and began to speak. The police were summoned, trooping into the main buildings for the first time in the Sorbonne's seven-hundred-year history. They arrested six hundred students, and when other young people swarmed through the neighborhood, known as the Latin Quarter, the government closed the university, another historic first.

The French president Charles De Gaulle, a popular military hero and dominating political figure, ridiculed the protest leaders, calling them poor students who were inspiring chaos so that they could avoid taking exams. Other government figures joined in belittling the student protesters. Alain Peyrefitte, the minister of education, offered this explanation: "Certain French students, having found out that students in other countries have shaken up and smashed everything, want to do the same."

On May 6, when Cohn-Bendit arrived to face the disciplinary board, students and police adversaries sized each other up throughout the university neighborhood. On one stretch of streets thousands of university students, now reinforced by high school youths, chanted their support for Cohn-Bendit. Roughly 1,000 troops from the national police force stood nearby, their long shields, dark clubs, and helmets giving them a menacing appearance.

The street fighting erupted with surprising force. Defying a government ban on demonstrations, thousands of students began marching and chanting. At one point, as a group of students turned onto the Rue St. Jacques, they were rushed by club-swinging police who knocked some down and forced others back. But the students regrouped, moving their positions and turning over parked cars to form barricades. Some began digging up cobblestones that were passed to strong-armed protesters up front so they could hurl them at the police. The fighting continued for hours. Later that night, the police reported that 600 protesters and 345 policemen had been injured.

In the days that followed, confrontations occurred all over the city. In the wave of violence, property was destroyed and people on both sides were hospitalized—but no one was killed.

For many French citizens, the idea of street battles evoked heroic scenes from French history. But there was also a noticeably contemporary aspect to the May events, which was reflected in thousands of posters that appeared around the city. As Dany le Rouge, or Danny the Red, Daniel Cohn-Bendit quite literally became the poster child for the movement when his beaming face appeared on thousands of silk-screened placards posted around the city.

None of the poster slogans quite rivaled the resonance of the country's old revolutionary rallying cry, "Liberty, Equality, Fraternity," but taken together they did express a great range of dissatisfaction, frustration, and anxiety, as well as whimsy. Posters declared, "Dreams are a reality," "A barricade closes the street but opens a path," "Politics happens in the street," "Imagination takes power," "I am a Marxist of the Groucho faction," and, "I have something to say but I am not sure what it is." A histo-

A poster depicts Daniel Cohn-Bendit, May 1968.

rian, Tony Judt, later wrote that one of the most striking things about the posters was that their authors "never invited people to do anyone serious harm." Judt noted that while televised scenes of aggressive police tactics did provoke widespread public disgust, "the May events had a psychological impact out of all proportion to their true significance."

At the time, as the television images raised

public indignation, a sense of crisis deepened by the hour and touched off demands for political action. At the outset, influential leaders—notably the heads of powerful Communist-led labor unions—supported De Gaulle and denounced the student leaders as "adventurists" and "anarchists." But as increasing numbers of both elite and ordinary Parisians objected to the heavy-handed conduct of the police, the Communists' position changed. Realizing that President De Gaulle and his prime minister, Georges Pompidou, were suddenly vulnerable, the labor leaders seized the opportunity to challenge the government's budget and to press for wage increases for French workers. Along with other labor leaders, they declared a one-day nationwide general strike for Monday, May 13.

On that day, France stopped. Millions of workers stayed home or took to the streets to demonstrate support for the students. More than a million people marched through Paris, where police kept a low profile and Pompidou personally announced the reopening of the Sorbonne and the release of the arrested students.

Yet when Tuesday arrived, it was clear that resentments lingered. The Sorbonne was reopened, but it was immediately seized by the students. More than four hundred action committees were set up throughout France to press grievances against the government. In many plants, strikers ignored union orders to return to work and either stayed away or staged sit-in strikes. The government authorized salary increases ranging from to 10 to 25 percent only to have them rejected by workers. Newspapers were describing a revolutionary fervor sweeping the country while commentators openly wondered how long the government could survive.

On May 30, more than 300,000 protesters participated in a union-led march through Paris during which many shouted, "Adieu, de Gaulle." The president, who in public statements had begun to look tired and uncertain, decided to address the nation the next day, speaking only on radio because state-run television was disabled by a strike. This time, he displayed his old political mastery, sounding again like the stern and resolute war hero that France had loved. Forcefully he declared that he was dissolving the National Assembly and ordering new elections to be held in three weeks. He demanded that workers return to their jobs and hinted of a military state of emergency if they did not.

The speech turned the tide. The strikes abated. The police retook the Sorbonne on June 16. The workers accepted increased wages. In the next election De Gaulle contended that France was threatened by Leftist totalitarianism

and that only he and his policies could save the country, as he had done before. Just before the elections another massive rally blocked traffic in much of Paris. This one was in support of De Gaulle, and more than a million people turned out. The Gaullists won an absolute majority, improving their position in the Assembly, while the Leftist parties lost half the seats they previously held.

As for Daniel Cohn-Bendit, after the disciplinary hearings, government authorities canceled his right to remain in France. Although he was born there, he was not a citizen because his parents were foreigners. He went to Germany, the country from which his Jewish parents had fled. There he taught school, won election to the Frankfurt city council, and later became a representative of the Green Party in the European Parliament.

Another small but significant consequence of the May events occurred in August of 1968. De Gaulle, eager to disarm any potential future uprising, ordered the cobblestone streets of the Latin Quarter repaved with asphalt.

A few years later in Paris, I bought a toy that had become the rage there—a soft rubber air-filled replica of a cobblestone that whistled when you squeezed it.

French riot police use cobblestones as a barricade during the protests, May 11, 1968.

"All the News
That's Fit to Print"

The New Y[ork]

VOL. CXVII . No. 40,310   © 1968 The New York Times Company.   NEW YORK, WE[D]

KENNEDY SHOT AND
AFTER WINNING CA
SUSPECT SEIZED IN

PRESIDENT INVITES SOVIET TO JOIN U.S. IN PEACE EFFORTS

Defends Policy in Address at Glassboro Commencement, Year After Kosygin Talks

Text of the Johnson speech appears on Page 14.

By MAX FRANKEL
Special to The New York Times

GL[ASSBORO], N.J., June 4

Marcus Testifies G.O.P. Official Urge[s] Him to Accept a Kickback on Contra[ct]

By BARNARD L. COLLIER

James L. Marcus took the witness stand yesterday and testified that Joseph E. Ruggiero, the Republican county law chairman, and Vincent Albano, the New York County Republican chairman, both had tried to induce him to award an $840,000 city contract to companies they favored.

The former Water Commissioner and once close adviser to Mayor Lindsay said in Federal court that on Nov. 17 or 18, 1966, he told his business partner and lawyer, Herbert

would go to Mr. Ruggiero and 5 per cent to Mr. Itkin and myself, and I felt that we ought to award the contract to Oakhill."

Testimony showed that the reference to "Oakhill" meant the Oakhill Contracting Company, Inc., of Queens, a concern that wanted the contract to clean and refurbish the Jerome Park Reservoir in the Bronx.

Marcus testified also that Mr. Albano had asked him to give the contract to a different company, S. T. Grand, Inc., because its owner, Henry Fried, "is a big contributor to the Republican

fore a 12-man jury h[as] evidence in United State[s] [Dis]trict Court in a bribery [con]spiracy trial. Marcus has [plead]ed guilty in the case to [taking] a bribe for awarding the [con]tract.

Marcus said that Mr. [Fried] who is not on trial no[w] was named as one of [the] co-defendants in the F[ederal] indictment handed up [last] December, was oppose[d] to making any deal with M[r. Rug]giero on the contract.

He quoted Mr. Itk[in as] saying:

"You've got to be cra[zy]

ork Times

continued warm tonight, tomorro .
Temp. range: today 83-58; Tues.
76-57. Temp.-Hum. Index 75; Tues.
70. Full U.S. report on Page 93.

DAY, JUNE 5, 1968

10 CENTS

GRAVELY WOUNDED
LIFORNIA PRIMARY;
LOS ANGELES HOTEL

OAST TALLY SLOW

ew Yorker Captures ead Over McCarthy n Late Tabulation

y LAWRENCE E. DAVIES
Special to The New York Times

LOS ANGELES, Wednesday,
ne 5—Senator Robert F.
nnedy defeated Senator Eu-
ne J. McCarthy yesterday in
lifornia's Democratic Presi-
tial primary.

After trailing in the vote
nt for several hours after
polls closed, Mr. Kennedy
ercame his rival in the tabu-
ion early this morning.

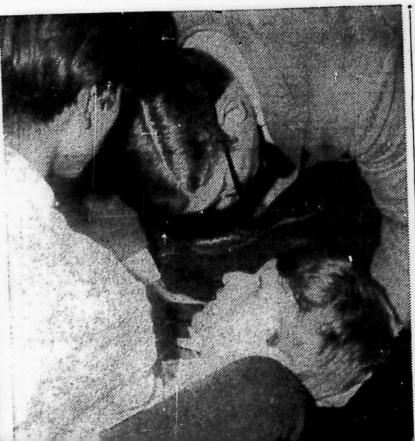

CONDITION 'STABLE'

Aide Reports Senator Is 'Breathing Well'— Last Rites Given

By WARREN WEAVER Jr.
Special to The New York Times

LOS ANGELES, Wednesday,
June 5—Senator Robert F. Kennedy was shot and critically
wounded by an unidentified
gunman this morning just after
he made his victory speech in
the California primary election.

Moments after the shots
were fired, the New York Senator lay on the cement floor of
a kitchen corridor outside the
h room of the Ambassador

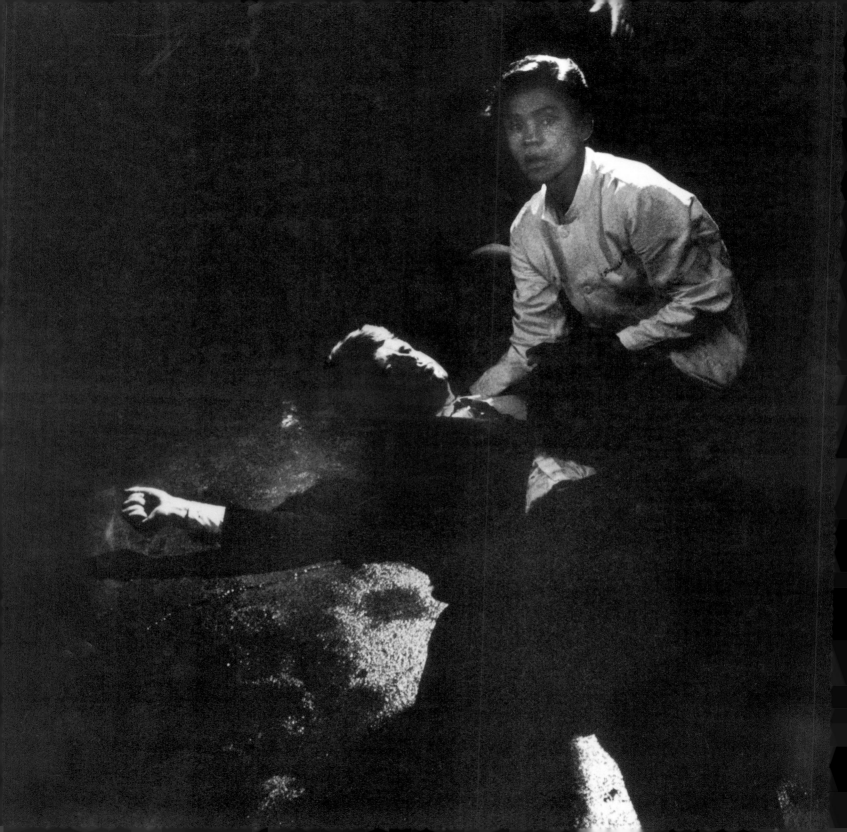

BOBBY KENNEDY

Paris calmed down quickly and world attention once more returned to Vietnam and its impact on the upcoming elections in the United States. On June 5, I arrived at the newsroom at seven-thirty P.M. to start work on the latest shift, which, for reasons I have never understood, is called the lobster trick. Normally as one of the latemen, I could expect to go home at three in the morning, when the last edition of the paper was put to bed. But that Tuesday evening I assumed I would be staying even longer, because it was the date of the Democratic primary in California.

Since West Coast time is three hours behind East Coast time, the paper would have to stay open longer than usual to wait for the results. The California contest was expected to decide whether Eugene McCarthy or Robert F. Kennedy would lead the antiwar wing of the Democratic Party. The winner of the contest would go on to confront Vice President Hubert H. Humphrey for the Democratic presidential nomination, to be decided at the August convention in Chicago.

For the previous six weeks, since the forty-two-year-old Kennedy had entered the race, the two men had waged an increasingly bitter struggle. McCarthy's enthusiastic young supporters regarded Kennedy as a Johnny-come-lately who had sat timidly on the sidelines while their man boldly took on Johnson and his war policies. For their part, Kennedy's backers depicted McCarthy as something of a modern-day Don Quixote, a mystical figure eager to confront evil in the abstract but lacking the resources, the contacts, the skills, and the gumption that their own champion flaunted. As he pressed his drive for the presidency, Robert Kennedy

Left: A busboy kneels over Robert F. Kennedy shortly after he was shot in the kitchen of the Ambassador Hotel, Los Angeles, June 5, 1968.

Previous page: *New York Times* front page from June 5, 1968. For full text of Bobby Kennedy article, see page 128.

BOBBY KENNEDY

In his brief but extraordinary political career, Robert Francis Kennedy was attorney general of the United States under two presidents and was a senator from New York. In those offices he exerted an enormous influence on the nation's domestic and foreign affairs, first as the closest confidant of his brother, President John F. Kennedy, and then, after Kennedy's assassination in 1963, as the immediate heir to his New Frontier policies.

The Kennedy name, which John had made magical, devolved on Robert, enabling him to win a Senate seat from a state in which he had little or no previous association. The Kennedy aura also permitted him to campaign for the Democratic presidential nomination and to gain important victories in the preference primaries. Wherever he went he drew crowds by evoking, through his Boston accent, his gestures, and his physical appearance, a remarkable and nostalgic likeness to his elder brother.

At the same time, Kennedy called forth sharply opposed evaluations of himself. For those who found him charming, brilliant, and sincerely devoted to the welfare of the country, there were others who vehemently asserted that he was calculating, overly ambitious, and ruthless.

Those who praised him regarded his candidacy for his party's presidential nomination as proof of his selflessness. They quoted with approval his announcement on March 16, in which he said:

I do not run for the presidency merely to oppose any man but to propose new policies. I run because I am convinced that this country is on a perilous course and because I have such strong feelings about what must be done, and I feel that I'm obliged to do all I can.

Kennedy was an indefatigable campaigner, able to put in a sixteen-hour day of stress and tension and then sleep briefly before going through another equally strenuous day. Indeed, he seldom seemed to relax, whether he was campaigning or not, for he played with as much concentration as he worked. He was, for instance, a vigorous touch football participant, a hardy skier, a pace-setting mountain climber, and a swimmer who did not mind plunging into the cold Pacific surf on an Oregon beach, an exploit few in that state ever attempted.

Kennedy was so constantly in motion that he prompted some observers to say that he fled introspection, that he did not want to sit down with himself and figure out what he truly was and what he wanted to achieve. He often conceded that he was aggressive, explaining semi-humorously:

"I was the seventh of nine children. And when you come from that far down, you have to struggle to survive."

was enchanting many Americans with what was sometimes called the "Kennedy magic," an emotional wave that had helped propel his older brother John F. Kennedy to the White House and persisted even after John was assassinated.

Bobby had been John's best friend, his confidant, and his campaign manager. As U.S. attorney general, he had lent support to an imprisoned Martin Luther King, Jr., and launched investigations into links between certain labor unions and organized crime. Throughout the 1960s, the American public had come to know the Kennedys through countless, usually admiring, magazine articles and television programs. In addition to the three political brothers—Jack, Bobby, and Teddy—there was Joe, the rich patriarch of the clan, who had steered his children toward prominence. Jacqueline, John's beautiful, elegant, and sophisticated wife, had become a fashion bellwether for millions of women. At the time of the California primary, Bobby's wife, Ethel, was expecting their eleventh child.

Prominent figures and stars from many fields were attracted to the Kennedys in such numbers that the White House during the Kennedy administration was often portrayed as a modern-day Camelot resembling King Arthur's legendary court. Now, as another charismatic Kennedy was seeking to win the White House, this influential battalion of movers and shakers—among them prizewinning historians, economists, and political scientists, and famous writers, singers, musicians, movie stars, and athletes—was returning to political battle and giving its powerful support to Bobby and his efforts to end the war.

As the primary season rolled on, the rivalry between the two peace candidates became increasingly bitter. McCarthy refused to meet with Robert Kennedy's younger brother, Ted. And when Kennedy's campaigners sought to stereotype McCarthy as a poetic scholar, the Minnesotan lashed back by trumpeting his own manliness. He declared, "[Kennedy] plays touch football; I play football. He plays softball; I play baseball. He skates in Rockefeller Center; I play hockey."

Throughout April, McCarthy followed up on his success in the New Hampshire primary by winning elections in Connecticut, Massachusetts, and Wisconsin, where Kennedy had entered the race too late to get on the ballots. The first contest in which the two men faced each other was in Indiana on May 7. There Kennedy won with 42.3 percent of the vote while McCarthy finished third behind the state's Democratic governor, Roger Branigan, who was running as a stand-in for Vice President Humphrey. A week later, Kennedy beat McCarthy in Nebraska by twenty percentage points.

The next face-off was in Oregon. A week before that vote Kennedy declared, "If I get beaten in any primary, I am not a very viable candidate." At that point Bobby Kennedy had won every election he had ever contested. But in Oregon, on May 28, his streak ended. McCarthy captured nearly 44 percent of the vote while Kennedy received 37 percent.

And then, five days later, came California. Because of its size and the number of votes it would have at the nominating convention, it was the most important showdown between the two men. If McCarthy were to win and build on his success in Oregon, he could seriously damage and possibly derail Kennedy's drive for the nomination and the presidency. If Kennedy won, he would be in an excellent position going into the primaries in New York and Florida.

On the night of June 4, I spoke by phone with the reporters in California and elsewhere and wrote several inserts that went into various by-now-forgotten stories. But I will always remember the moment, shortly after three A.M. in New York—midnight in Los Angeles—when I learned that Bobby Kennedy had been shot. I was on the phone with Larry Davies, one of the reporters in Los Angeles, taking down the four or five paragraphs he was dictating to replace the beginning, or "top," of his earlier story about the contest. It was the paper's leading story, the one at the far top right of page one. The earlier versions had Kennedy leading; the new top had him the winner.

I typed as fast as I could. Mike Boylan, the national desk clerk, stood by my desk waiting to rush the page to the copyeditors so they could get the words into print as quickly as possible. The phone at the empty desk next to mine rang. Boylan picked it up and the caller said: "This is Wally Turner. Kennedy's been shot."

Wallace Turner was one of the *Times*'s California correspondents, but Boylan had never spoken to him and couldn't recognize his voice. The television sets, which were on, were not mentioning any shooting, and Boylan understandably wondered whether the call might be a hoax. Politely he asked the caller if he could name the paper's national editor. "Ray O'Neil," Turner answered correctly, and Boylan transferred the call to the senior editors. Minutes later, at exactly 3:22, the presses were shut down.

From that moment, everyone—the reporters in Los Angeles and other cities, the editors, and our rewrite crew—went into high gear to prepare the report that would appear in the 240,000 copies of the Wednesday morning *Times* that started rolling off the presses at 5:58 A.M., New York time. That edition described how Senator Kennedy, after claiming victory and thanking his campaign workers, was leaving the Ambassador Hotel in Los Angeles through a kitchen pantry when he was shot. The gunman, captured after firing eight shots that wounded five people besides Senator Kennedy, would soon be identified as Sirhan Sirhan, a twenty-four-year-old Palestinian who resented Kennedy for his support of Israel. The headline stretching across the full width of the paper declared:

KENNEDY SHOT AND GRAVELY WOUNDED AFTER WINNING CALIFORNIA PRIMARY; SUSPECT SEIZED IN LOS ANGELES HOTEL

Sirhan Sirhan is led away after shooting Robert F. Kennedy, June 6, 1968.

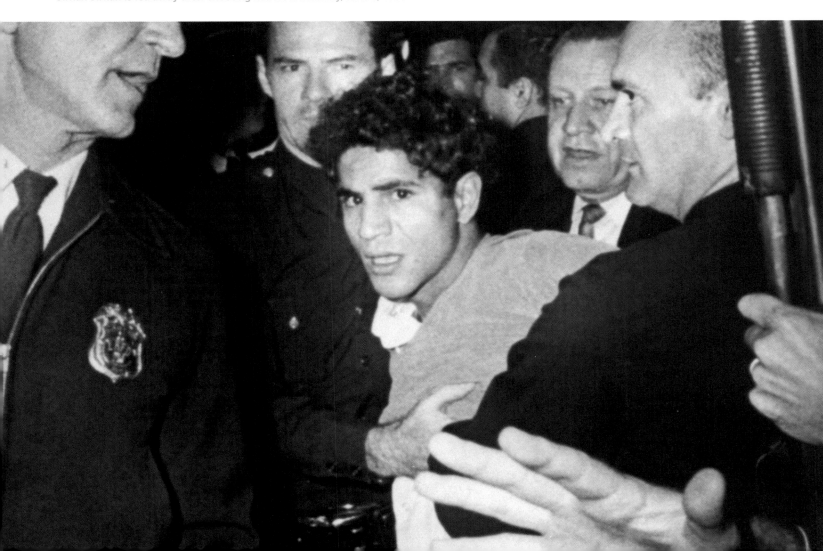

Robert Kennedy died from his wounds in the Good Samaritan Hospital in Los Angeles at 1:44 A.M. on June 6.

A terrible sense of loss and mourning settled over much of the nation as Robert F. Kennedy's body was carried home by train. People stood by the tracks in reverent, often tearful silence as the funeral carriage passed. The shock and sadness extended to people of all parties who were powerfully touched by an awareness that Robert Kennedy, so closely linked to his brother John by blood, politics, and ambition, was now also tied to him by the violence of his death.

Within this huge mass of mourners there were many people who viewed the killing as a dreadful political as well as human tragedy. They included antiwar activists, political liberals, proponents of expanded civil rights, labor union members, ethnic minorities, young people, feminists, and others who believed deeply that the achievement of their respective goals and agendas had depended on getting Robert Kennedy elected as president.

A crowd watches the train carrying the body of Bobby Kennedy through Rahway, New Jersey, June 8, 1968.

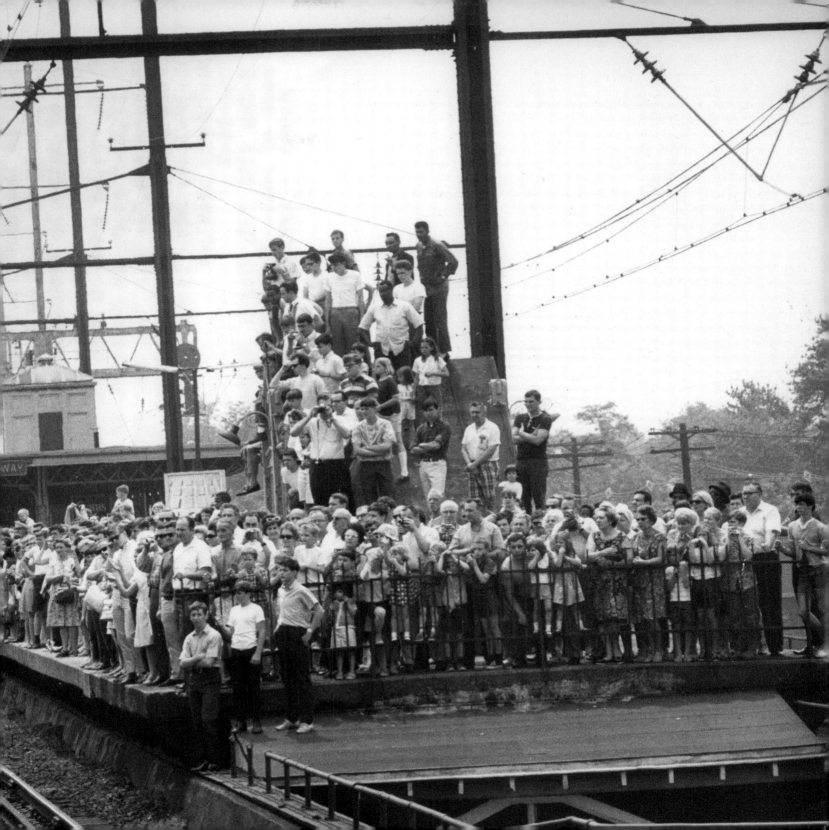

VOL. CXVII . No. 40,387

© 1968 The New York Times Company.

NEW YORK, WED

CZECHOSLOVAKIA IN
AND FOUR OTHER W
THEY OPEN FIRE C

13 INDICTED HERE IN RIGGING OF BIDS ON UTILITY WORK

Contracts Worth 49-Million Involved—14 Construction Companies Also Named

By MARTIN TOLCHIN

Fourteen major construction companies, 12 top corporate

Democrats Debate Position on the War in Vietr

ork Times

seasonable tonight and tomorro
Temp. range: today 89-73; Tuesda
91-72. Temp.-Hum. Index yesterda
81. Complete U.S. report on Page 9

Y, AUGUST 21, 1968

10 CENT

VADED BY RUSSIANS
RSAW PACT FORCES;
CROWDS IN PRAGUE

OVIET EXPLAINS

ays Its Troops Moved at the Request of Czechoslovaks

RAYMOND H. ANDERSON
Special to The New York Times

MOSCOW, Wednesday, Aug.
— Moscow announced this
orning that troops from the
oviet Union and four other
ommunist countries had in-
aded Czechoslovakia at the
equest of the "party and Gov-
leaders of the Czech-

TANKS ENTER CI'

Deaths Are Report —Troops Surroun Offices of Party

By TAD SZULC
Special to The New York Times

PRAGUE, Wednesday,
21—Czechoslovakia was c
pied early today by troop
the Soviet Union and fou
its Warsaw Pact allies
series of swift land and
movements.

Airborne Soviet troops

PRAGUE

Throughout the first half of 1968, much of the world news had been focused on the Vietnam War. Except for the flurry of strikes in France in May, events in Europe had not commanded great attention. Some speculated that the long cold war rivalry between Moscow and Washington might be entering a new, less dangerous phase. In July came a historic announcement that the United States and the Soviet Union had agreed to hold talks aimed at limiting and reducing the nuclear weapons that the two states were aiming at each other.

There was much discussion of achieving *détente,* a French word that refers to a period of reduced tension between countries that have previously been in conflict. But toward the end of August, those hopes suddenly and surprisingly capsized when, shortly before midnight on August 20, the Soviet Union launched a major invasion of its Communist ally Czechoslovakia. Soon after dawn on August 20, 165,000 troops and 4,600 tanks crossed Czechoslovakia's borders from every direction, quickly occupying the East European country of 12 million people, and took up positions at railroads, highways, schools, factories, and government offices.

The attack came without warning, either within Czechoslovakia or in Western capitals. The first edition of *The New York Times* for August 21 rolled off the presses with no mention of any military threat or action, though a front-page story from Moscow noted that an on-again, off-again dispute between Communist leaders in Moscow and Prague was intensifying.

Then, after the early edition was being printed, Allan Siegal, the late-night editor

Left: Residents of Prague go about their business as Soviet tanks occupy the streets.

Previous page: *New York Times* front page from August 21, 1968. For full text of Czechoslovakia article, see page 130.

ALEXANDER DUBČEK

Almost immediately upon succeeding Antonin Novotny as first secretary of the Czechoslovak Communist Party in January 1968, Dubček began to loosen the stringent control that had defined Communist political life in Eastern Europe under the dominant influence of the Soviet Union. He quickly found himself in confrontation with the Kremlin.

He had previously been known as a loyal Communist with strong party credentials, and was regarded as a shy man, certainly not one given to impulsive action.

Within weeks of taking office, however, Dubček stunned Moscow and the rest of the world with his publicly stated determination to achieve the "widest possible democratization" of Czechoslovakia and the establishment of "a free, modern, and profoundly humane society."

And he sent out word that the purges and political vendettas of the past were to be no more.

When other Warsaw Pact nations denounced his behavior as unacceptable, the Czechoslovak Communist Party's Central Committee announced rather nervously that Dubček's liberal moves would only strengthen the nation's ties to the rest of the Warsaw Pact nations.

On August 21, 1968, armed forces from the Soviet Union, Hungary, Poland, East Germany, and Bulgaria invaded Czechoslovakia. After the invasion, Dubček was expelled from the party and dispatched to Turkey, where he served as Czechoslovak ambassador to Ankara. Then, in June 1970, he was banished to an even more obscure job dealing with forestry in his native Bratislava, and there he remained until 1987.

In November 1989, he reappeared in Czechoslovak national life, delivering a speech before a huge rally in Bratislava, as the wave that would sweep Communism from power reached its crest in nationwide strikes and demonstrations. Dubček backed Vaclav Havel, the playwright who had been jailed by the Communists, and his so-called Velvet Revolution. On the night Havel was elected president, the playwright introduced Dubček on the balcony overlooking Wenceslas Square.

The man who was ahead of his time and not forgotten by his people was unanimously elected speaker of Parliament, as Havel became president. At his death in 1992, Dubček was the leader of Slovakia's Social Democrats.

In the years following 1968, Dubček said that he would do it over again if given the chance. He said that he had never feared for his life, but in describing his feelings when he thought of all that had happened to the people of Czechoslovakia, he said, "Tears come to my eyes easily."

on the foreign desk, noticed a bit of copy from the Soviet Tass news agency reporting that Soviet forces, backed by troops of four other Communist countries, had been sent to provide "fraternal assistance" to the people of Czechoslovakia. It was around nine P.M. in New York, or three A.M. Wednesday morning in Prague and five A.M. in Moscow. Siegal quickly phoned Moscow to wake Ray Anderson, the *Times's* correspondent, and inform him of what had happened. Anderson rapidly put together a story but was forced to stew anxiously as he failed to get a phone line, a common problem in those days. After a few hours Siegal managed to get through to Anderson and have rewrite pick up his story. Meanwhile Tad Szulc (pronounced "Shultz"), the *Times's* man in Prague, also succeeded in finding a working phone and transmitting his account of the Soviet occupation as it was taking place around him.

In less than six hours, *Times* staffers produced eleven articles that appeared on two and a half full pages of the final edition covering the late-breaking developments in Czechoslovakia. While the outcome of the invasion was then far from clear, there was little doubt that the events unfolding in Prague were becoming one of the most important stories in a year filled with so many big stories. The headline on the final edition declared:

CZECHOSLOVAKIA INVADED BY RUSSIANS AND FOUR OTHER WARSAW PACT FORCES; THEY OPEN FIRE ON CROWDS IN PRAGUE

The political tensions that triggered the invasion had been building over the previous seven months. It had all started back in January, when Antonin Novotny, the long-ruling Communist Party boss of Czechoslovakia, was replaced by a younger man, Alexander Dubček. Dubček was a tall, plainspoken, and modest figure, who though devoted to Communist ideology favored more open debate and greater public discussion of policies.

His ideas of building "Socialism with a human face" attracted attention and wide popular support, as did his proposals for easing the strict censorship that Czechoslovakia's Communist leaders had imposed and enforced. One of his early reforms permitted foreign newspapers to be sold freely. Another allowed the country's writers' association to publish a journal with articles on previously forbidden subjects. The national radio began airing diverse viewpoints that went beyond the previous echoing of the party's positions.

Encouraged by this new permissiveness, Czechoslovakian society grew more assertive. Western clothes such as jeans and miniskirts that had been officially scorned now became desirable. Western popular music—from jazz to blues and rock—which had been denounced as decadent, was gaining popularity. Within months of Dubček's taking over as party chief, the national mood had shifted from grim austerity to an era of playful experimentation and innovative and provocative writing. The period would come to be known as "the Prague Spring." Czechoslovakia, with its architecturally imposing cities, excellent beer, and fine music, was becoming a tourist magnet, making it virtually the only destination on the other side of the Iron Curtain that attracted large numbers of young Western visitors.

All of this change alarmed the Communist bosses of the Soviet Union and Czechoslovakia's other neighbors—Poland, East Germany, and Hungary. For these leaders, any reform was viewed as potentially troublesome, something that might lead to instability or even rebellion against the Soviet-led Communist camp. They all remembered the Hungarian uprising of 1956, when the Red Army had fought street battles in Budapest to violently suppress a reform movement. More recently, in May of 1968, hard-line Polish Communists had cracked down harshly on university students who were demanding greater freedom. For the old-fashioned Communist leaders, social ripples like the Prague Spring were regarded as dangerous and potentially contagious.

Two months before the invasion, rumors had briefly circulated about menacing Soviet troop movements. Leonid Brezhnev, the Soviet leader, spoke out pointedly about the need to "defend Socialism," the same phrase the Soviets had used in 1956 to justify their invasion of Hungary. Then for four days in the middle of the summer, Brezhnev had visited with Dubček in a town near the Ukrainian border. When those talks ended, Dubček delivered a televised address on August 2 assuring the Czechoslovakian people that the country's self-rule was not imperiled. He added that Czechoslovakia's ultimate independence required good relations with the Communist leaders in Moscow, and he urged citizens to show restraint and discipline when discussing the Soviets. Commentators inside and outside Czechoslovakia concluded that Dubček, while slowing down the reforms, had prevailed and that the crisis had passed.

Eighteen days later, Russian forces backed by smaller units of Polish, East German, Hungarian, and Bulgarian troops launched the largest and most complex Soviet-led military operation since the Second World War.

Soon after the troops moved, Czechoslovak radio kept repeating a bulletin in which Dubček and his associates announced that the country had been invaded without their knowledge.

They appealed "to all citizens of [the] republic to maintain calm and not to offer resistance to the troops on the march." Some young people ignored the urgings and threw rocks and Molotov cocktails—glass bottles filled with gasoline and ignited with wicks of flaming rags—at the Soviet troops and tanks. But mostly the angry crowds either sat down in front of the tanks or taunted the foreign soldiers using the Russian they had been forced to learn in school, shouting for them to go home.

Dubček spent the night at his office in the Central Committee building, which Soviet troops had encircled and to which the phone lines had been cut. At nine o'clock in the morning, paratroopers rushed the building, seized

Students in Prague heckle Soviet soldiers, August 1968.

Dubček, and flew him and his key associates to a KGB barrack in Soviet Ukraine. The Soviets believed that with Dubček out of the way, the Czechoslovak Central Committee would quickly bow to necessity and vote to replace their leader with someone who was more acceptable to Moscow.

But this did not happen. Instead, television footage of Czechoslovaks resisting the occupiers made its way out of the country. The Soviet claims that their troops had been first invited and then welcomed were revealed as lies. Dozens of Communist parties, including those of France and Italy, joined Western democracies in denouncing the invasion. Soviet embarrassment deepened as Moscow failed to find any credible Czechoslovakians willing to express appreciation for the "fraternal assistance" they were extending.

At one point Soviets tried to turn to Ludvik Svoboda, a seventy-two-year-old war hero whose position as Czechoslovakia's president was mostly ceremonial. Svoboda, who had gained his reputation fighting against the Nazis in World War II, had been critical of Dubček and the Prague Spring. Yet when a group of Moscow's Czechoslovakian operatives urged him to sign a declaration endorsing the Soviet occupation, the old patriot rose from his desk and chased his visitors, shouting, "Get out!"

The Soviets then switched tactics, bringing Dubček and his associates to Moscow for discussions. The men's haggard and nervous appearance testified to the hardship of their imprisonment. Dubček, who had a gash on his forehead, was pale and had difficulty speaking. Later reports suggested that he had been drugged and forcibly sedated. For several days the Soviets and the Czechoslovaks faced each other across a table, with Dubček struggling to defend the reforms and Brezhnev attacking them as dangerous to Moscow and the entire Soviet Bloc.

Meanwhile, Soviet troops took full control of Czechoslovakia, killing seventy-two citizens and wounding more than seven hundred others. The Czechoslovakian leaders who had been roughed up and intimidated continually refused to approve of the invasion. But as virtual prisoners in Moscow, they were powerless to withstand Soviet pressure and they ultimately agreed to sign a document known as the Moscow Protocol, an ambiguously worded proclamation urging Czechoslovakia to move toward "normalization," a term that was generally understood to mean a return to hard-line policies and an end to "the spring."

On August 27, Dubček returned to Prague. In the month that followed, measures were imposed to cancel press freedoms and restore

Soviet troops march through Prague, September 10, 1968.

censorship. Seven months later, in April of 1969, he was forced out as party secretary, and in 1970 he was expelled from the party.

But that is not quite the end of the story. In 1984, sixteen years after the Prague Spring was crushed, I became the *Times*'s Eastern Europe correspondent. For almost four years, while based in Warsaw, I would regularly visit Czechoslovakia. It seemed to me that of all the Soviet satellite countries I covered it was Czechoslovakia that was the most obedient and docile. I often visited with Václav Havel, a dissident playwright who was constantly being shadowed by government agents. He agreed that Czechs were submissive with the Soviet Union, but at the same time he urged me to be more understanding of how heavily the shock of 1968 still weighed upon his countrymen. They had tasted liberty in that short period of springtime, and they still carried psychological wounds from the invasion. But Havel would also insist that deep in their hearts the citizens of Czechoslovakia still clung to hopes

first aroused during the Prague Spring. I was inspired but not entirely convinced, particularly when I realized how isolated Havel seemed. Even his neighbors refused to acknowledge his greeting when he met them on the staircase.

Then, just three years later, I was forced to recall Havel's observations. It was December of 1989 and I was back in New York as the deputy foreign editor, helping to coordinate the *Times*'s coverage of the collapse of Communist rule in Eastern Europe. In Czechoslovakia, what became known as the Velvet Revolution triumphed remarkably, without bloodshed. At least 250,000 people turned out in Wenceslas Square to cheer a new democratic government that was headed by Václav Havel. They also cheered wildly for a smiling sixty-eight-year-old man who was standing next to Havel on the high balcony. Though the man had spent the last two decades as an obscure employee of the Bratislava office of the forestry department, everyone in the square and in the country knew that it was Alexander Dubček.

Alexender Dubček salutes the crowd at Wenceslas Square upon his return to Prague, November 24, 1989.

HUMPHREY BARS RIGI[]
AND FLOUTING OF LA[]

CZECHS TO RENEW CURBS ON PRESS AND NONRED CLUBS

Smrkovsky Discloses Plan for Restraint on Reform Under Moscow Pact

Excerpts from speech giving terms of accord, Page 2.

By TAD SZULC
Special to The New York Times

PRAGUE, Aug. 29—Plans to restore press censorship and disband non-Communist political groups were announced here today as the first steps to restrain Czechoslovakia's democratic reform in the wake of last week's invasion by the

Moscow Says Foes Peril Czech Accord

By HENRY KAMM
Special to The New York Times

MOSCOW, Aug. 29 — The Soviet Union charged today that "counterrevolutionary forces" in Czechoslovakia were trying to frustrate the carrying out of the obligations Czechoslovakia undertook in her negotiations with the Soviet Union.

These negotiations, which concluded here Tuesday, provided for restraints on the democratization program.

In a situation report published by Tass, the official press agency, Moscow accused unidentified counterrevolutionaries of attacking the leaders of the Czechoslovak party and Government in an attempt to seize power.

During the Moscow negotiations, the Soviet Union ac-

THOUSANDS MARCH

Scores Are Arrested, Some Delegates— Tear Gas Is Used

By J. ANTHONY LUKAS
Special to The New York Times

CHICAGO, Friday, Aug. 30— More than 150 people, including nine convention delegates, were arrested last night after National Guardsmen halted 3,000 persons marching toward the International Amphitheatre.

The guardsmen then fired tear gas to disperse the rest of the crowd. Later they fired more tear gas into ranks of demonstrators in front of the Conrad Hilton Hotel.

The first canisters of gas arched into crowds on Michigan Avenue at exactly 10:30 P.M.,

AUGUST 30, 1968

10 CENTS

71-61. emp.-Hum. Index yesterday
70. Complete U.S. report on page 66.

...TY IN VIETNAM POLICY
MUSKIE ON HIS TICKET

RIOTING ASSAILED

2 Nominees Speak at Tumultuous Final Session of Parley

Text of Humphrey's speech is printed on Page 17.

By TOM WICKER
Special to The New York Times

CHICAGO, Aug. 29—Hubert H. Humphrey accepted the Democratic Presidential nomination tonight with a promise that on the issue of Vietnam "the policies of tomorrow need not be limited by the policies of yesterday."

In an emotional speech interrupted 75 times for applause, with some boos heard on three occasions, Mr. Humphrey pledged to unify his divided party and nation and call them to a "new sense of purpose..."

CHICAGO

In the last week of August, as Soviet tanks patrolled Czechoslovakian cities, angry, mostly young American war protesters rallied on the streets of Chicago, where the Democratic Party was meeting to nominate its presidential candidate. After many of the young people were beaten, arrested, and tear-gassed, some accused the city's mayor and police of violently crushing their rights of free speech and assembly, and they referred to the city as "Czechago," and "Prague West."

And just as television images from Prague had been watched by an enormous audience, so too were millions of Americans watching a riveting and violent television drama that combined scenes of angry debate inside the convention hall with coverage of turmoil on nearby streets.

Inside the International Ampitheater, delegates were selecting the man who would run against Richard M. Nixon, who had been chosen as the Republican candidate in a cut-and-dried convention in Miami Beach twenty days before. Since the assassination of Bobby Kennedy, supporters of Vice President Hubert H. Humphrey had faced off against those committed to Senator Eugene McCarthy and another more recently declared antiwar contender, Senator George McGovern of South Dakota.

On Wednesday, August 28, the delegates heatedly debated which of two rival positions on Vietnam policy should be included in the party's platform. The first plank (called the "hawk plank" by its opponents) supported the Johnson administration's position that the

Left: Delegates at the 1968 Democratic Convention carry signs to protest the Johnson/Humphrey policy on the Vietnam War.

Previous page: *New York Times* front page from August 30, 1968. For full text of Chicago convention article, see page 132.

RICHARD M. NIXON

Richard Milhous Nixon's tumultuous political career was born in the anti-Communist fervor of the cold war. In the early days of that struggle and afterward, he employed slashing tactics that provoked strong emotions among voters.

Combative, suspicious, and sometimes vengeful, Nixon was a fiercely partisan Republican as a representative and then as a senator from California in the late 1940s and early 1950s, as vice president under President Dwight D. Eisenhower from 1953 to 1961, and as president from 1969 to 1974.

Vietnam gave him his opening. The unpopularity of the war forced Lyndon B. Johnson to the sidelines and obliged his would-be heir, Hubert H. Humphrey, to run the race carrying a backbreaking handicap. But Nixon proved a strong enough candidate to exploit the opportunity, winning a narrow victory.

Four years later, a tide of votes from those whom he called "the silent majority" gave him one of the great election sweeps in American history. He carried forty-nine states, losing only Massachusetts and the District of Columbia.

But less than two years later, he became the only president in more than two centuries of American history to resign from office. He was driven from office by the Watergate scandal, resigning in the face of certain impeachment on August 9, 1974. His face wet with tears, he bade the remnants of his broken administration goodbye with words that seemed to draw a moral from his own searing experience: "Always remember, others may hate you, but those who hate you don't win unless you hate them, and then you destroy yourself."

He often acknowledged that the event would inevitably stain his pages in history, and despite strenuous and partly successful efforts over two decades to rehabilitate his reputation, he was right.

Yet Nixon, surely one of the half-dozen pivotal figures of American politics in the quarter-century that followed World War II, wrought foreign policy accomplishments of historic proportions that had proved beyond the reach of his Democratic foes.

He reopened American relations with China in 1972. He began the rapprochement with the Soviet Union with the signing of the first treaty limiting the potentially deadly nuclear arms race. And after at first broadening and intensifying the conflict in Vietnam, he ended American involvement in the fighting there.

bombing of North Vietnam should continue until Hanoi accepted conditional terms. This document, essentially dictated by the White House, was backed by the party's bosses—most prominently, Mayor Richard Daley of Chicago. The alternate proposal, referred to as the doves' plank, had been drafted by supporters of Senator McCarthy and Senator McGovern and by people close to Robert Kennedy. In addition to calling for an unconditional suspension of bombing, that plank urged that the United States press the South Vietnamese to negotiate directly with the North Vietnamese for "a broadly representative government in Saigon."

The debate, lasting three hours, was intense. Shouts of "Stop the war!" rang out, and at one point most of the New York delegation rose to sing "We Shall Overcome." In the end, the delegates voted to reject the doves' plank by 1,567 to 1,041.

Meanwhile, an antiwar rally was getting under way in Grant Park near the convention hall. Months earlier leaders of various antiwar groups—including the Students for a Democratic Society, the mischievous and anarchistic Yippies, the Black Panther party, and even veterans of an Old Left group called the War Resistors League—had discussed mounting a mass antiwar protest in Chicago during the convention. Mayor Daley grew alarmed by the

prospect—he was eager that his city look well run to the millions of Americans who would be watching the convention on television. In the weeks before the convention he repeatedly declared, "Law and order will be maintained," and he saw to it that permit requests for protest marches were denied. He imposed an eleven P.M. curfew for the convention week. Police had their days off canceled and were ordered to work expanded shifts, with large numbers of them positioned throughout the Loop, as the downtown area of Chicago is known. They were reinforced by National Guardsmen assigned to further shield the convention site.

In the end, as a later official inquiry showed, no more than 5,000 demonstrators arrived from out of town. Despite the nervous precautions, the rally at Grant Park began whimsically when demonstrators nominated a pig named "Pigasus" for president and the rock band MC-5 played. Then, as speakers denounced Mayor Daley and President Johnson, three young men began hauling an American flag down from a pole near the park's band shell. According to the eyewitness accounts of *New York Times* reporters, a group of blue-helmeted police rushed in to stop the young men but were kept from the flagpole by the crowd. More officers stormed in from the edge of the crowd, and one launched a tear gas canister. A demonstrator picked it up and heaved it back toward the police. The crowd began cheering.

Knots of demonstrators faced off against clusters of police. Rocks were thrown and nightsticks were swung. The poet Allan Ginsburg took the microphone to urge calm, declaring, "The best strategy for you in cases of hysteria, overexcitement, or fear is to chant 'om' together. It helps to quell flutterings of butterflies in the belly. Join me as I now try to lead you."

Many in the crowd chanted and the police stepped back as speakers including the writers Norman Mailer and William S. Burroughs addressed a crowd that has been estimated at between 5,000 and 10,000 people. After a relatively peaceful interlude, people began drifting across the street to the Hilton Hotel, where both McCarthy and Humphrey had their headquarters. Television sets at street level were showing what was happening inside the convention center, where by that time state delegations were being polled on their choices for the nomination. Each time Humphrey's total rose the crowd booed loudly.

Chicago police attack antiwar demonstrators on Michigan Avenue, Chicago, August 28, 1968.

Then all hell broke loose. Some of the demonstrators began heading toward the convention center. In *The Times,* reporter J. Anthony Lukas described what happened:

The police and guardsmen used clubs, rifle butts, tear gas and chemical Mace on virtually anything moving along Michigan Avenue and the narrow streets of the [downtown] Loop Area.

Even elderly bystanders were caught in the police onslaught. At one point, the police turned on several dozen persons standing quietly behind police barriers, in front of the Conrad Hilton Hotel watching the demonstrators across the street.

For no reason that could be immediately determined the blue-helmeted policemen charged the barriers, crushing the spectators against the windows of the Haymarket Inn, a restaurant in the hotel. Finally the window gave way, sending screaming middle-aged women and children backward through the broken shards of glass. The police then ran into the restaurant and beat some of the victims who had fallen through the windows and arrested them.

Just as the demonstrators had learned from television what was going on at the convention, the delegates at the convention learned what was taking place on the street by watching TV coverage. One of the most memorable moments of the convention came as Senator Abraham Ribicoff of Connecticut, a supporter of Senator McGovern, offered a speech in which he declared: "With George McGovern as president of the United States we wouldn't have Gestapo tactics in the streets of Chicago." The cameramen instantly pivoted their lenses to focus on Mayor Daley, who was seen standing in the aisle surrounded

Chicago Mayor Richard Daley shakes his fist while listening to Connecticut Governor Abraham Ribicoff's speech, August 28, 1968.

by heavyset bodyguards, shaking his fist menacingly at Ribicoff and shouting. The sound was not picked up, but to many lip-reading viewers, it seems that Daley was shouting obscenities at Ribicoff.

Though the convention week's violence ended without anyone being killed, 668 people were arrested, more than 100 civilians were treated at hospitals, and more than 1,000 others were cared for by volunteer physicians at street clinics. One hundred and ninety-two police officers reported injuries. Three months later, a national commission on the causes and prevention of violence issued a report claiming the disorders centered on what was termed a "police riot."

Any list of the week's more seriously harmed victims would have to include both Hubert H. Humphrey and the Democratic Party. Though Humphrey coasted to the nomination with twice as many votes as McCarthy and McGovern combined, it was clear he was heading into battle against Richard Nixon with his own party in visible disarray. The chances of Humphrey, once regarded as a social progressive, winning over the energized young people who had flocked to McCarthy, McGovern, and Kennedy were exceedingly slim. Moreover, as Lyndon Johnson's vice president, he could not easily disassociate himself from White House

policies on Vietnam. Coming out of Chicago, Humphrey had slightly more than two months left before Election Day to try to heal the party divisions that had been so graphically revealed by the mayhem at the convention.

The Republican candidate, Richard Nixon, on the other hand, was sailing into the final phase of the campaign season with a cohesive and expanding constituency. Nixon was eager to disprove the author F. Scott Fitzgerald's much-quoted line about there being "no second acts in American lives." Six years earlier, Nixon, who had served as vice president under Dwight D. Eisenhower and then lost a presidential race to John F. Kennedy in 1960, failed to make a comeback when voters rejected his bid to become governor of California. At that time he bitterly addressed reporters, saying, "You won't have Nixon to kick around anymore, because, gentlemen, this is my last press conference."

There had been a long intermission, but his second act was off to a promising start. In addition to the divisions among the Democrats, Nixon was shrewdly pursuing what came to be known as the "southern strategy." For a hundred years since the Civil War, the Republican Party, which had been the party of Abraham Lincoln and the party of post–Civil War Reconstruction, had held very little appeal for southern whites. But Nixon realized that significant numbers of southern whites had felt alienated from the Democratic Party after Johnson pushed through civil rights legislation. Through his choice of Spiro Agnew, the tough-talking governor of Maryland, as his running mate—and by his own emphasis on restoring "law and order" and "respecting states rights"—Nixon was actively targeting southern whites while projecting himself as a mainstream moderate in other parts of the country.

The race for president was further complicated by the third-party candidacy of George Wallace, the former governor of Alabama, whose appeal to the racism of some southern whites was neither subtle nor nuanced. Wallace, after all, was the man who on winning the Alabama governorship in 1962 had unabashedly uttered his most famous words: "I draw the line in the dust and toss the gauntlet before the feet of tyranny, and I say segregation now, segregation tomorrow, segregation forever."

On November 7, 1968, Richard Milhous Nixon won the presidency, narrowly defeating Hubert Horatio Humphrey in the popular vote but comfortably outpolling him in the electoral vote.

As was the case with many of the occurrences of 1968, the American political dramas of that year set in motion a chain of events that would continue to play out for decades. For example, Nixon's southern strategy would help Republicans win six of the next nine presidential contests. And even though Nixon would be forced out of office during his second term under threat of impeachment, the country continued to drift to the right politically, with more and more people identifying themselves as conservatives and fewer as liberals. The separations of society that became so evident in 1968 on the streets of Chicago would persist until the present, with rival commentators portraying the period around 1968 as either an era of heightened democracy, personal freedom, and youthful energy or as a time of turmoil in which national unity was destroyed, traditional values discarded, and discipline tossed out the window.

Richard Nixon campaigns for the presidency in California, September 17, 1968.

VOL. CXVIII..No. 40,430

ST. LOUIS WINS, 4-0, IN SERIES OPENER; GIBSON SETS MARK

Cardinal Hurler Strikes Out 17 Tigers to Break Record of 15 Held by Koufax

---

M'LAIN LEAVES IN SIXTH

Winners Score Three Runs in Fourth—Brock Clouts a Home Run in Seventh

---

By JOSEPH DURSO
Special to The New York Times

ST. LOUIS, Oct. 2 — Bob Gibson outpitched Denny Mc-Lain, overpowered the rest of the Detroit Tigers and struck out 17 batters today as the St. Louis Cardinals won the opening game of the World Series, 4-0.

The 32-year-old Nebraskan broke the Series strike-out record of 15, set by Sandy Koufax of the Los Angeles Dodgers

Handshake for Great Performance

Bob Gibson, Cardinals' pitcher, being congratulated by Tim McCarver after striking out 17 in St. Louis yesterday.

Associated Press

AT LEAST 20 DEA AS MEXICO STR REACHES A PE

Troops Fire Machine and Rifles at Student More Than 100 Hu

By PAUL L. MONTGOM
Special to The New York Time

MEXICO CITY, Oct. 2—eral troops fired on a s rally with rifles and m guns tonight, killing at 20 people and wounding than 100.

The troops moved on of 3,000 people in the sq a vast housing project night was falling. In an of firing that lasted an the army strafed the are machine guns mounted and tanks.

About 1,000 troops to in the action. Tanks, a cars and jeeps followe spurting .30- and .50 machine-gun fire.

Buses, trolley cars an vehicles were set on fire eral places in the city. lances screamed thro

Temp. range: today 73-65, Wea.
85-66. Full U.S. report on Page 93.

OCTOBER 3, 1968

10 CENTS

viet Diplomats Hear Moscow Denounced at U.N.

The New York Times (by Carl T. Gossett Jr.)

akov A. Malik, left, chief Soviet representative at the U.N., and Andrei A. Gromyko,
oviet Foreign Minister, listen as Secretary of State Dean Rusk addresses U.N. General
ssembly. Mr. Rusk assailed the Soviet bloc for its military action in Czechoslovakia.

ENATE REJECTS MISSILES DELAY

Rusk, at U.N., Reaffirms NATO's Defense of Bonn

Paris Accuses Moscow

FORTAS ABANDONS NOMINATION FIGHT; NAME WITHDRAWN

Justice, in Letter to Johnson, Says Senate Attacks Might Mar Court's New Term

DILEMMA FOR PRESIDENT

He May Try Another Man, Risking a Second Rebuff, or Yield to Successor

Texts of Fortas letter and Johnson statement, Page 42.

By FRED P. GRAHAM
Special to The New York Times

WASHINGTON, Oct. 2—Associate Justice Abe Fortas withdrew today as President Johnson's nominee for the office of Chief Justice, clearing the way for the President to submit a possible second nomination to the Senate.

In a letter that concluded with a prayer for "fairness and justice and moderation," Jus tice Fortas asks Mr. Johnso

MEXICO CITY

For several years, the Mexican president Gustavo Díaz Ordaz had been looking forward to October 1968 as the month when his place in Mexican history would be assured. In October, the summer Olympic Games were scheduled to take place in the thin air of mile-high Mexico City. But the students and young people of Mexico City, like young people in Paris and on the streets of Chicago, had their own, very different priorities.

For years Díaz Ordaz and the Institutional Revolutionary Party, or PRI, which had long run Mexico, had waged a diplomatic campaign to have their country chosen as the first Latin American country to host the Olympics. When the city had finally been chosen, an ambitious period of preparation had begun. Arenas, stadiums, swimming pools, hotels, an athletes' village, and new roads were designed and constructed. Massive art projects by world-class artists, both foreign and Mexican, were completed to show off the country and its capital city, then one of the world's fastest-growing metropolises.

Díaz Ordaz and his party believed that if the Olympics went well, the event would convince the world of Mexico's transformation from a picturesque but rural and poor nation into a fully modern state, with expanding industrial and economic power and impressive cultural resources. The country would be able to attract more foreign investment to sustain its growth.

Mexican leaders had high hopes that everything would work out, but they were keeping their fingers crossed against crisis. Early in the year they had experienced a scare when the

Left: Mexican protestors burn the Soviet flag to protest the invasion of Czechoslovakia, August 29, 1968.

Previous page: *New York Times* front page from October 3, 1968. For full text of Mexico City article, see page 136.

GUSTAVO DÍAZ ORDAZ

Gustavo Díaz Ordaz, the austere, tough-minded judge and politician who as president of Mexico led the bloody suppression of student riots in 1968, was born March 12, 1911, in what is now Serdan, state of Puebla. The son of a government accountant and a schoolmistress, he worked his way through Puebla University and, after earning his law degree, became a court clerk and then a judge.

He gained a reputation as a labor-law specialist while serving as president of Mexico's Central Council of Conciliation and Arbitration. When he entered politics, he was assistant to the governor of Puebla, then became a member of the lower house of parliament and a senator from Puebla. He was named to a post of the Interior Ministry in 1952, and six years later was made interior minister.

Díaz Ordaz began his six-year term as president in 1964 with a reputation as a hard-working, middle-of-the-road leader who would tolerate extremists of neither the right nor the left.

A stern and serious man, Díaz Ordaz was known for putting in long hours with only short breaks in his rigorous official schedule.

While in the cabinet of his predecessor, President Adolfo Lopez Mateos, he was in charge of internal security and was thus one of the most influential men in the government. He was criticized by the left for cracking down on its radical elements. But it was the severe response to the student unrest in Mexico City in 1968 that roused worldwide attention and reproach.

Its memory continued to provoke strong reactions in Mexico long after Díaz Ordaz was succeeded by his interior minister, Luis Echeverria Alvarez, in 1970. When Díaz Ordaz was appointed ambassador to Spain in 1977, the Mexican diplomatic corps became sharply divided over the choice, and the Mexican press reprised its criticism of how he had handled the confrontation with the students.

International Olympic Committee had ruled to reinstate South Africa. That country had been banned from participation in the previous Olympics because of its policy of apartheid, the strictly enforced separation of black and white South Africans. The decision to allow South Africa's participation in Mexico City had led groups and individuals in a number of countries to consider a call for a boycott of the games by teams, tourists, or individual athletes. One of the most energetic supporters of a boycott was Harry Edwards, a black professor of sociology from California, who for a number of years had encouraged black athletes to consider how they might advance civil rights and black solidarity.

By summer the threat of any large-scale boycott in Mexico had evaporated, though some African countries declined to send teams. But the fear of embarrassing protests continued to trouble Mexican authorities. They had paid careful attention to what had happened at Columbia University in April, on the streets of Paris in May, and in Chicago in August. They also may have been aware of protests that had been staged in the United States for women's rights. In Atlantic City, New Jersey, on September 7, just six weeks before the Olympic Games were to begin, some four hundred women protesters had turned up outside of the theater where the Miss American Pageant was being held, with signs declaring, "No More Beauty Standards" and "Welcome to the Cattle Auction." They put up a "Freedom Trash Can" into which women had tossed items such as false eyelashes, wigs, curlers, fashion journals, men's magazines such as *Playboy,* high-heeled shoes, and bras. Although the protest was not widely supported, it turned out to be a major early success for the women's movement, drawing lasting media attention and instigating debate on the roles of women in modern societies.

Much more than issues of race or gender, the primary concern of Mexican officials during the countdown to the Olympics centered on the behavior of Mexican university students. All through the spring and summer, students had held rallies on a variety of themes. Some expressed sympathy for French students, support for the Cuban revolution, and solidarity with Czechoslovakian youth. Silk-screened posters like those in Paris began to appear around the city.

By the beginning of August, students from a number of schools in the capital organized a national strike council, whose program was similar to one the Students for a Democratic Society circulated at U.S. campuses, including Columbia University. Generally they called for greater democratic choices, less control by the ruling party, more open debate, less censorship, and expanded freedom of expression. At the end of August, as many as 100,000 people were marching in student-led processions in the capital, and protests were spreading to other cities.

On the first day of September, Díaz Ordaz delivered the annual presidential speech to the nation. In it, he noted that his government had been criticized for "excessive leniency" in dealing with the student protests. Sternly he added, "There is a limit to everything and the violations of law and order that have occurred recently before the very eyes of the nation cannot be allowed to continue." Then he warned, "We will do what we have to do."

On September 18, army units with armored vehicles surrounded the main campus of the National Autonomous University of Mexico. Some reports said that as many as 1,000 students and teachers were arrested. Five days later, on September 23, police and the army invaded the National Polytechnic Institute, where students fought back, and uniformed forces fired at the students. *The New York Times* reported that forty students were wounded, while the Mexican press provided scant details.

On October 2, government officials met with the strike committee in an attempt to calm things down—but nothing was achieved.

Within hours of the meeting, the conflict reached its dramatic and tragic climax in an ancient market square, the Tlatelolco, where some 450 years earlier Aztec rule had been violently crushed by Spanish conquistadors. The square's old name had been changed to the Plaza of the Three Cultures, a reference to the three ethnic strands of modern Mexico: the original Indians, the Europeans, and the Mestizo offspring of the two.

The students had called the rally for four in the afternoon. Compared to earlier demonstrations, the turnout was relatively small, with the crowd of students and some union workers numbering between 4,000 and 5,000. Soon after the first of the speakers began addressing the crowd from a large third-floor balcony, army helicopters began hovering overhead. In addition to the student leaders and their supporters, the balcony was also filling up with young men in civilian clothes wearing conspicuous white gloves. Later, many who were there told stories of sudden machine-gunfire. Some of these witnesses described how the men in the white gloves fired down on the crowd. Meanwhile, uniformed soldiers who were positioned among the unarmed people on the plaza floor began shooting at the balcony to return the fire of the white-gloved snipers.

University students are held inside an apartment building in Tlatelolco, Mexico City, October 2, 1968.

At ground level, sections of the crowd raced in panic toward a church, only to find its doors barred. According to witnesses cited by historians, the firing continued for two and a half hours.

Even today, four decades later, the details and the statistics of the Tlatelolco Square incident have never been fully established. Later works of historical and journalistic inquiry disclosed that the shooters on the balcony were members of a military unit that reported to the president. What is clear is that the gunfire claimed a significant though still unconfirmed number of lives. On the day after the event, Mexico City and foreign newspapers provided differing tolls, with one major Mexican daily claiming that twenty-nine people were killed and eighty wounded, while another reported that one general and eleven uniformed soldiers had been wounded by snipers and more than twenty civilians were killed. *The New York Times* said that "at least twenty were killed," and the British *Guardian* newspaper reported that 325 people had been killed. That is also the figure cited by the writer Octavio Paz, who resigned as a Mexican diplomat to protest the shootings.

The shootings brought the student movement to an abrupt halt. There were no more protests or demonstrations, and ten days after the killings the Olympics opened right on schedule. There were no boycotts and almost all the events went off smoothly and without controversy. Except for one remarkably iconic and photogenic exception.

In the final heat of the two-hundred-meter race, the American runners Tommie Smith and John Carlos finished first and third. Both were from San Jose State in California, where they had frequent discussions with Harry Edwards, their teacher and friend, about how black athletes might express support for black causes. So in their moment of glory, as they stood on the platforms with the gold and bronze medals hanging from their necks and as the national anthem of the United States played, Smith and Carlos stood solemnly with their arms held over their heads, their hands clenched in fists. One raised his right arm, the other his left, and both fists were covered with leather gloves. The idea, they later explained, was that the salute conveyed black power and the use of both left and right arms suggested black unity.

Photographs and television images of the scene quickly circulated around the globe, and controversy erupted. Avery Brundage, the head of the American Olympic Committee and

Students arrested in a roundup following the October 2 massacre, October 3, 1968.

the man most instrumental in bringing South Africa back into the Olympics, quickly expelled the two champion runners from the American team and the Olympic Village, claiming their gesture had violated some Olympian ideal by making a political statement. Back in the United States, the men were initially subjected to widespread criticism, almost exclusively from whites, and they even received death threats. In time the controversy died down and the two runners generally gained increasing respect.

Over time the events at the Plaza of Three Cultures tarnished the reputations of Mexican politicians and contributed to the eventual decline of the once invincible PRI. In the end, Díaz Ordaz's place in Mexican history was determined more by what took place in the plaza than by his economic policies or his role in bringing the Olympics to Mexico.

In 1971, a Mexican writer and journalist named Elena Poniatowska published a book, *La Noche de Tlatelolco* (called *Massacre in Mexico* for the English translation) that provided testimony about the shooting from many people who were there. The book continues to have a profound impact on Mexican society.

The political sensitivities about Tlateloclo and the causes of the tragedy were so great that for twenty-five years no monument could be constructed at the site. It was 1993 before the government allowed the placement there of a commemorative stone mentioning the lives lost and the blood spilled.

U.S. athletes Tommie Smith (center) and John Carlos, winners of the 200-meter gold and bronze, raise their gloved fists while receiving their medals, October 16, 1968.

3 MEN FLY ARO
ONLY 70 MILES
FIRE ROCKET,

PUEBLO CREWMEN GREETED ON COAST; CAPTORS ASSAILED

Relatives Weep and Scream —Captain Asserts North Koreans Are Inhuman

By BERNARD GWERTZMAN
Special to The New York Times

Pope Paul Says Mass In a Huge Steel Mill

By ROBERT C. DOTY
Special to The New York Times

TARANTO, Italy, Wednesday, Dec. 25—Pope Paul VI celebrated Christmas midnight mass here for 15,000 workers and members of their families in a huge, echoing rolling mill.

The Pontiff chose the vast Italsider steel plant at this developing industrial center in the heel of the Italian boot as the place to express "the

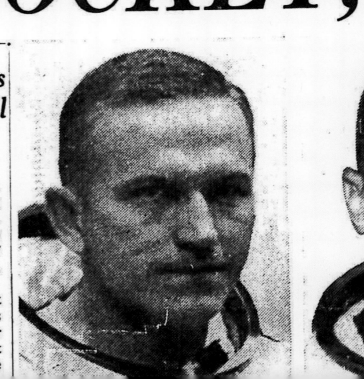

Temp. range: today 30-20; Tuesday
34-24. Full U.S. report on Page 62.

DECEMBER 25, 1968   10 CENTS

ND THE MOON
ROM SURFACE;
EAD FOR EARTH

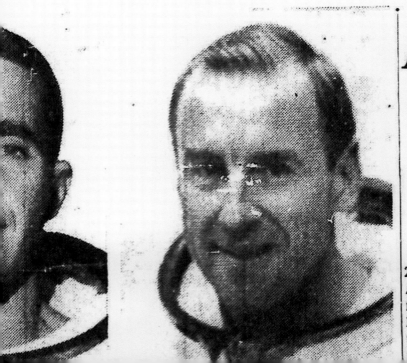

Astronauts Examine 'Vast, Lonely' Place; Read From Genesis

By JOHN NOBLE WILFORD
Special to The New York Times

HOUSTON, Wednesday, Dec. 25—The three astronauts of Apollo 8 yesterday became the first men to orbit the moon. Early today, after flying 10 times around that desolate realm of dream and scientific

dirty beach sand with lots of footprints on it" and said it "looks like plaster of Paris."

At about 9:30 P.M. the astronauts began their second and last television show from lunar orbit. It ran some 30 minutes

APOLLO

It was now winter. The year that had started with the intensified violence of the Tet Offensive and had proceeded through traumatic assassinations, riotous upheavals, and the invasion of a small country by a large superpower, was nearly over. People were preparing to look backward as the New Year approached. This time they would be able to do so from a totally new perspective.

As 1968 drew to a close, the Apollo 8 space mission soared into the heavens to circle the moon. Scarcely two days into the flight, on the day after Christmas, the three-man crew beamed back the first images of our planet ever to be seen by human beings. It was an awesome sight, transmitted live to millions of television viewers around the world and inspiring many responses that underscored the season's conventional hopes for peace on earth and goodwill toward men.

Archibald MacLeish, one of America's best-known poets of the period, observed in a front-page article in *The New York Times,* "that to see the earth as it truly is, small and blue and beautiful in that eternal silence where it floats, is to see ourselves as riders on the earth together, brothers on that bright loveliness in the eternal cold—brothers who know now they are truly brothers."

Another poet who wrote about Apollo 8 was Ann Morrow Lindbergh, whose husband, Charles Lindbergh, had pioneered the age of flight in 1927 when he flew a small plane alone across the Atlantic from New York to Paris. Forty-one years after his triumph, she suggested how our newly available views of the world

Left: NASA astronauts Frank Borman, William Anders, and Jim Lovell.

Previous page: *New York Times* front page from December 25, 1968. For full text of Apollo 8 article, see page 137.

might change human behavior. "As earthmen," she wrote, "we may have taken another step into adulthood. We can see our planet earth with detachment, with tenderness, with some shame and pity, but at last also with love."

I vividly remember being one of the millions who were thrilled by those televised images of our globe. I also remember wanting to share in the hopes raised by the poets and to believe that earthlings everywhere might now be moved to view the planet as our common home and to treat each other with tenderness and love and brotherhood. But to tell you the truth, the way 1968 had gone, there seemed very little reason for optimism. However tranquil and comforting the world may have looked from the vicinity of the moon, from my vantage point at *The New York Times,* the year then drawing to an end had been violent, stormy, and tragic. Frank Borman, the commander of the Apollo 8 mission, had hinted as much after he landed. He acknowledged, "The view of the Earth from the Moon fascinated me—a small disk, 240,000 miles away," but then he added, "Raging nationalistic interests, famines, wars, pestilence, don't show from that distance."

Throughout 1968, all the troubles that the commander mentioned, and many others as well, had been clearly visible at ground level. Even now, forty years later, I still think of that year as one in which the flow of bad news never slackened. In my memory, 1968 persists as a year unlike any other: the culmination of the turbulent 1960s, a terrible and shocking time. For a young newsman, it was addictively exciting. It seemed that the whole world was battered by one unexpected and menacing event after another. Everywhere you looked there was "bang bang," which is how we on the rewrite team referred to those episodes of newsworthy troubles that kept erupting. As human beings we feared and were repelled by "bang bang," but as reporters we were attracted, and wanted to witness it up close.

Looking back, I now realize how so many trends and events that came later—both good and bad—were set in motion or accelerated by what occurred in that twelve-month period. From national politics in the United States, to tensions within the Communist bloc, to the conduct of war and the prospect of peace and nuclear arms control, to progress on civil rights and the growing power of young people and women, 1968 was a critical turning point. It had been both terrifying and exciting, a truly unforgettable year.

One of the first images taken of the earth from space, transmitted December 24, 1968.

ARTICLES

STREET CLASHES GO ON IN VIETNAM, FOE STILL HOLDS PARTS OF CITIES
By Charles Mohr

SAIGON, South Vietnam, Friday, Feb. 2—Vicious street fighting continued today in many South Vietnamese towns and cities, and the Vietcong attacked three more province capitals.

The United States military commander, Gen. William C. Westmoreland, said yesterday that there was some evidence that the enemy's general offensive was "about to run out of steam," but he also conceded that the enemy had a capability to continue "this phase of their campaign for several more days."

[The United States command announced that 10,593 enemy soldiers had been killed since 6 P.M. Monday—by far the heaviest losses ever inflicted by the allies in Vietnam, United Press International reported. American losses were put at 281 killed and 1,195 wounded and South Vietnamese losses at 632 killed and 1,588 wounded.]

SOME QUESTION TOTALS
The assertion today that more than 10,000 of the enemy had died in the outbreaks was viewed with reserve by some observers. One, a press release, said that in a fight near Pleiku in the central highlands, 208 of the enemy were killed and one Vietnamese militiaman wounded.

Since Monday, the Vietcong have attacked 26 of the country's 44 province capitals, penetrating some of them deeply.

New attacks were reported yesterday and today on the towns of Baria, Muchoa and Phucuong, all province capitals. Other important cities, such as Danang, have also been attacked in the Vietcong drive.

Five battalions of Vietcong and North Vietnamese troops were still fighting heavily within the walls of the ancient citadel at Hue, the former imperial capital.

Strong government forces have broken into the citadel to relieve troops who had held out in the South Vietnamese First Division compound within its confines.

Tenacious guerrilla forces were holding out in the important Mekong Delta towns of Mytho and Bentre, 40 and 55 miles south of Saigon. Vietnamese sources said the guerrillas were using the girls' high school as a command post in Mytho and that there was heavy fighting at the bus station this morning.

The United States Navy river patrol base near the delta town of Vinhlong had to be abandoned after Vietcong units overran that province capital.

One battalion of South Vietnamese troops was reported to be holding out in its compound in the city but was said to be "heavily engaged." Rescue forces were on their way.

ATTACKS REPULSED

Government sources said the attacks on the towns of Baria, east of Saigon, and Phucuong, to the northwest, had been repulsed eventually. But two Government tanks were destroyed in Baria and two armored cars in Phucuong.

Thirty Government soldiers died and 57 were wounded in the battle for Phucuong yesterday. They said they had killed 80 Vietcong.

On the outskirts of Saigon, two platoons of regional-force militia fled their post at an important bridge on the highway to nearby Bienhoa, the site of a major United States base, when guerrillas attacked.

The 38th South Vietnamese Ranger Battalion counterattacked and retook the bridge, Government sources said.

Sniping continued on a scattered scale in parts of Saigon and its Chinese quarter, Cholon. The Vietcong entered some houses in Cholon last night and sent the residents out to bring back food.

At 4 A.M. today a mortar and rocket attack was made on a United States supply company depot near the Saigon dock area. There was no immediate damage or casualty report.

KHESANH ATTACK PREDICTED

General Westmoreland said at his news conference yesterday that the enemy's "main effort" would be a big attack at or near the United States Marine outpost at Khesanh, near the borders of Laos and North Vietnam.

Discussing the enemy, who has massed 20,000 to 40,000 troops opposite the 5,000 marines, General Westmoreland commented, "I give him the capability of attacking in force at any time in the Khesanh area." But except for sporadic shelling from enemy guns and rockets, Khesanh remained quiet, as it had for several days.

The fighting in Saigon was aimed at wiping out the remnants of some five battalions—2,000 to 2,500 men—that entered the city Wednesday. Some of the sharper Saigon fighting occurred near the city's Tansonnhut air base.

In one incident yesterday, Government troops in Saigon broke into the An Quang pagoda, headquarters of the anti-Government faction of Vietnamese Buddhism, after getting reports that a sizable force of infiltrated guerrillas was inside. Only nuns, monks and children were found, witnesses said, but guerrillas were killed and captured in nearby residential buildings.

The Vietcong had occupied the compound of a South Vietnamese army tank unit in the city and had beheaded one officer. They executed several women and children among the families of officers.

One South Vietnamese major, who helped retake his living quarters in fierce fighting, wept as he carried one of his dead children out of the area.

The Vietcong and the North Vietnamese are believed to have about 100 "combat effective" battalions, totaling 50,000 rifleman, in South Vietnam. A military official said that most of these units had been committed to the offensive that began Monday and that the rest were ready for quick use.

The total does not include the troops around Khesanh.

M.P. BILLET SEIZED

Dalat, a mountain resort that is a favorite hideaway of South Vietnamese generals, was entered by the Vietcong. They seized an American military-police billet and controlled the central market, firing at "targets of opportunity," a military spokesman reported.

Troops of the United States' First Cavalry Division (Airmobile) were reported to have retaken Quangtri, the northernmost province capital in South Vietnam, after two battalions of enemy troops had overrun part of it.

Kontum, a mountain town near the border with Laos, was still partly in the hands of enemy forces, but the Vietcong troops had apparently eased their pressure on another mountain town, Banmethuot, the capital of Darlac Province.

"This is a terrible loss of face for the Government," an informed Vietnamese said. "Many people are very discouraged."

Premier Nguyen Van Loc announced that censorship would be imposed on South Vietnamese newspapers. In a reversal of an earlier decision, workers in Saigon were told to stay home today. A nationwide state of martial law was declared yesterday.

General Westmoreland said the Vietcong were paying a very heavy price for the political and psychological impact of their offensive.

The general said it would take "many, many weeks" and enemy units to regain full fighting strength.

General Westmoreland made it clear that he believed the wave of attacks on populated areas was only a phase of a general enemy strategy that would culminate with a large attack on Khesanh and on the whole of the two northernmost provinces, Quangtri and Thuathien.

The general indicated that he believed the campaign had been planned in Hanoi. He said it signaled an abandonment of the usual principle of protracted warfare followed by Communist guerrillas.

According to Lieut. Gen. Fred C. Weyand, commander of American forces in the 11 provinces surrounding Saigon, Vietcong prisoners captured in Saigon had been told to take objectives in the city and holdout for 48 hours, "until relieved" by reinforcements.

General Weyand, who is considered one of the most thoughtful students of the war in Vietnam, suggested that the offensive grew out of a basic change of the Vietcong's strategy aimed at correcting what he called "the degradation of their influence among the population."

For much of last year, he said, the Vietcong tried to avoid heavy, costly fighting with American and South Vietnamese units. But the national election in the fall, he said, "convinced them they had to do something about the slipping influence with the population."

Putting forth an opinion shared by General Westmoreland, General Weyand recalled that the Vietcong first staged a series of dramatic attacks in such isolated border areas as Locninh and Dakto late last year. One aim, he said, was to force the American commanders to deploy troops away from populated areas.

Soon afterward, General Weyand asserted, the Vietcong began reinforcing their "regional" units near Saigon and other cities and reorganized their diffuse capital into five pie-shaped units, all pointed toward coordinated attacks.

General Weyand said that he had become aware of this reorientation of enemy thinking and that, to meet it, by the middle of January he had withdrawn American units from search-and-destroy missions in remote areas. At least 85 percent of the American troops under his command were then returned to duty in populated areas, the general said.

Intelligence reports indicated a strong likelihood of a Vietcong attack on towns during the period of Tet, the Lunar New Year, and on Monday night General Weyand ordered all units into a "maximum alert posture."

Nonetheless by Tuesday morning, large enemy forces had infiltrated Saigon. In a guerrilla war such infiltrations can never be prevented. While the population did not stage an uprising to welcome the Vietcong, General Weyand conceded that local guerrilla units had "performed an invaluable service" in guiding main units through the thin screen of South Vietnamese security forces around Saigon.

While saying that the Vietcong had failed to capture almost all of their military objectives in the attacks, General Weyand conceded the Vietcong had concentrated on "remunerative" objectives of political and psychological warfare. This is the point of the new strategy, he said.

JOHNSON SAYS HE WON'T RUN
By Tom Wicker

WASHINGTON, March 31 —Lyndon Baines Johnson announced tonight: "I shall not seek and I will not accept the nomination of my party as your President."

Later, at a White House news conference, he said his decision was "completely irrevocable."

The President told his nationwide television audience:

"What we have won when all our people were united must not be lost in partisanship. I have concluded that I should not permit the Presidency to become involved in partisan decisions."

Mr. Johnson, acknowledging that there was "division in the American house," withdrew in the name of national unity, which he said was the "ultimate strength of our country."

"With American sons in the field far away," he said, "with the American future under challenge right here at home, with our hopes and the world's hopes for peace in the balance every day, I do not believe that I should devote an hour or a day of my time to any personal partisan causes or to any duties other than the awesome duties of this office, the Presidency of your country."

HUMPHREY RACE POSSIBLE
Mr. Johnson left Senator Robert F. Kennedy of New York and Senator Eugene J. McCarthy of Minnesota as the only two declared candidates for the Democratic Presidential nomination.

Vice President Humphrey, however, will be widely expected to seek the nomination now that his friend and political benefactor, Mr. Johnson, is out of the field. Mr. Humphrey indicated that he would have a statement on his plans tomorrow.

The President informed Mr.

Humphrey of his decision during a conference at the latter's apartment in southwest Washington today before the Vice President flew to Mexico City. There, he will represent the United States at the signing of a treaty for a Latin-American nuclear-free zone.

SURPRISE TO AIDES
If Mr. Humphrey should become a candidate, he would find most of the primaries foreclosed to him. Only those in the District of Columbia, New Jersey and South Dakota remain open.

Therefore, he would have to rely on collecting delegates in states without primaries and on White House support if he were to head off Mr. Kennedy and Mr. McCarthy.

Former Vice President Richard M. Nixon is the only announced major candidate for the Republican nomination, although Governor Rockefeller has said that he would accept the nomination if drafted.

Mr. Johnson's announcement tonight came as a stunning surprise even to close associates. His main political strategists, James H. Rowe of Washington, White House Special Assistant W. Marvin Watson, and Postmaster General Lawrence F. O'Brien, spent much of today conferring on campaign plans.

They were informed of

what was coming just before Mr. Johnson went on national television at 9 P.M. with a prepared speech on the war in Vietnam.

As the speech unfolded, it appeared to be a strong political challenge to Mr. Kennedy and Mr. McCarthy, announcing measures that they had been advocating.

The President thus seemed to be acting in the political tradition of his office—demonstrating that his was the power to act while his critics had only the power to propose.

But Mr. Johnson was really getting ready to place himself in a more obscure tradition—that Vice Presidents who succeed to the Presidency seek only one term of their own. Before him in this century, Theodore Roosevelt, Calvin Coolidge and Harry S Truman followed that pattern.

"WILLING TO PAY ANY PRICE"

Mr. Johnson ended his prepared speech and then launched into a peroration that had not been included in the printed text and the White House sources say he had written himself.

He began by quoting Franklin D. Roosevelt: "Of those to whom much is given—much is asked."

He could not say that no more would be asked of Americans, he continued, but he believed that "now, no less than when the decade began, this generation of Americans is willing to pay any price, bear any burden, meet any hardship, support any friend, oppose any foe, to assure the survival and the success of liberty."

This quotation from a celebrated passage of John F. Kennedy's inaugural address of Jan. 20, 1961, appeared to be a jab at Senator Robert F. Kennedy who now is campaigning against the war in Vietnam.

The ultimate strength of America, Mr. Johnson continued, in the rather funereal voice and with the solemn expression that he had maintained throughout his 40-minute speech, is not powerful weapons, great resources, or boundless wealth but "the dignity of our people."

He asserted again a political philosophy he has often expressed—that he was "a free man, an American, a public servant and a member of my party—in that order—always and only."

In his 37 years of public service, he said, he had put national unity ahead of everything because it was true now as it had ever been that a house divided against itself by the spirit of faction, of party, of religion, of race, is a house that cannot stand."

Mr. Johnson spoke proudly of what he had accomplished in the "52 months and 10 days" since he took over the Presidency, after the assassination of John F. Kennedy in Dallas, Tex., on Nov. 22, 1963.

"Through all time to come," he said. "I think America will be a stronger nation, a more just society, a land of greater opportunity and fulfillment because of what we have all done together in these years of unparalleled achievement."

"Our reward," he said, "will come in a life of freedom and peace and hope that our children will enjoy through ages ahead."

"But these gains, Mr. Johnson said, "must not now be lost in suspicion and distrust and selfishness and politics . . . I have concluded that I should not permit the Presidency to become involved in the partisan divisions that are developing."

And so it was that the man who won the biggest political landslide in American history when he defeated Senator Barry Goldwater of Arizona in the Presidential election of 1964, renounced the idea of a second term.

In American politics, a "draft" could override even words as strong as Mr. Johnson's, and he did stop short of the ultimate denial—the assertion that he would not run if nominated nor serve if elected.

But the first reaction of close associates and of other political observers here was that he meant what he said. Moreover, the candidacies of Senator Kennedy and Senator McCarthy would make a draft even of an incumbent President virtually impossible.

ROOSEVELT MOVE RECALLED

Still, if Vice President Humphrey does not enter the race, suspicion will undoubtedly be voiced that Mr. Johnson is trying to stimulate a draft.

Some observers with long memories recall that in 1940, President Franklin D. Roosevelt had Senator Alben W. Barkley of Kentucky read the Democratic National Convention a message in which Mr. Roosevelt said that he had "never had, and has not today, any desire or purpose to continue in the office of President, to be a candidate for that office, or to be nominated by the convention for that office."

The convention nonetheless nominated Mr. Roosevelt for a third term, and he won.

Mr. Roosevelt was not opposed for nomination by any candidate considered as powerful as Senator Robert Kennedy, however. In addition Senator McCarthy appears likely to win the Wisconsin primary on Tuesday, after having made a strong showing in New Hampshire.

The low point to which Mr. Johnson's political fortunes have fallen was dramatized in a Gallup Poll published today. It showed that his conduct of his office had the approval of only 36 percent of those polled, while his handling of the war in Vietnam was approved by only 26 percent.

The war was unquestionably the major factor in Mr. Johnson's slump in public esteem. He began a major escalation in February, 1965, by ordering the bombing of Northern Vietnam, just a few months after waging a Presidential campaign in which he had convinced most voters that he would not expand what was then a conflict involving only about 16,000 noncombatant American troops.

Over the years since then, the war has required a commitment of more than half a million combat troops, an expenditure of about $30 billion a year and heavy American casualties.

It limited Mr. Johnson's expenditures for domestic programs, alienated many of his supporters in Congress and provoked widespread and sometimes violent dissent—including draft card burnings, a march of thousands on the Pentagon last year, and ultimately the candidacies of Senators Kennedy and McCarthy.

"A NASTY FIGHT" SEEN

Nevertheless, a close political associate of the President said tonight that Mr. Johnson had by no means been "forced" out of the race by his opponents, nor was it yet clear that he would fail to win renomination.

"It was going to be a nasty fight but he had a good chance to win it," was his summation of the political situation. He said that one factor in Mr. Johnson's decision probably was that "this war's upset the hell out of him" and as a result he "really didn't have his mind on politics."

There was some speculation tonight that Mr. Johnson might believe he could work more effectively for peace in Vietnam if he were not a partisan candidate for re-election—despite the "lame duck" status that would confer on him.

Senator Albert Gore, Democrat of Tennessee, an old antagonist of Mr. Johnson, said the withdrawal was "the greatest contribution toward unity and possible peace that President Johnson could have made."

To achieve peace, he said, would require "concessions and compromises which would subject a candidate for public office to the charge of appeasement, surrender and being soft on the Communists."

In support of this thesis, Mr. Johnson's speech on Vietnam—which came before his withdrawal announcement—was notably conciliatory, although Senator Gore pointed out that "the President did not reveal a change in war policy tonight. He discussed only tactics—a partial bombing halt."

Theodore White the journalist interviewed Mr. Johnson earlier this week and is reported to have said later that the President's remarks had a "valedictory" tone.

Others who have talked with the President lately have detected a note of "they can't take this away from me" when he discussed his domestic and other achievements.

There was little insight here tonight on why Mr. Johnson chose to announce a withdrawal rather than to fight for renomination. One clue may have been in the theme of national unity on which he chose to base his announcement.

Almost since he took office, and at least until the political pressures generated by the war in Vietnam became intent, Mr. Johnson had sounded that same theme of unity.

Early in his Presidency, he seemed to have built a "consensus" of Americans that was reflected in the more than 60 percent of the vote he won in 1964.

As a reflection of that vote, he could work in 1965 and 1966 with a heavily Democratic, remarkably liberal Congress that passed some of the most far-reaching social legislation of the post-war era—medical care for the aged, voting rights for Southern Negroes, Federal aid to education, and a sweeping Civil Rights package.

UNITY THEME RECALLED

Mr. Johnson campaigned on a unity theme in 1964 and as far back as when he was the Democratic leader in the Senate, from 1952 to 1960, he frequently appealed for "closing ranks" and for "working together."

Thus he was eminently qualified to say, as he did tonight that "as President of all the people, I cannot disregard the peril to the progress of the American people and the hope and the prospect of peace for all people. So I would ask all Americans whatever their personal interest or concern to guard against divisiveness and all of its ugly consequences."

On that note, Mr. Johnson took his own personal step to "guard against divisiveness."

He surprised everybody, the way he always likes to do, and it probably pleased him most that the news did not leak out before he announced it himself.

MARTIN LUTHER KING IS SLAIN IN MEMPHIS
By Earl Caldwell

MEMPHIS, Friday, April 5—The Rev. Dr. Martin Luther King Jr., who preached nonviolence and racial brotherhood, was fatally shot here last night by a distant gunman who then raced away and escaped.

Four thousand National Guard troops were ordered into Memphis by Gov. Buford Ellington after the 39-year-old Nobel Prize–winning civil rights leader died.

A curfew was imposed on the shocked city of 550,000 inhabitants, 40 percent of whom are Negro.

But the police said the tragedy had been followed by incidents that included sporadic shooting, fires, bricks and bottles thrown at policemen, and looting that started in Negro districts and then spread over the city.

WHITE CAR SOUGHT
Police Director Frank Holloman said the assassin might have been a white man who was "50 to 100 yards away in a flophouse."

Chief of Detectives W. P. Huston said a late model white Mustang was believed to have been the killer's getaway car. Its occupant was described as a bareheaded white man in his 30s, wearing a black suit and black tie.

The detective chief said the police had chased two cars near the motel where Mr. King was shot and had halted one that had two out-of-town men as occupants. The men were questioned but seemed to have nothing to do with the killing, he said.

RIFLE FOUND NEARBY
A high-powered 30.06-caliber rifle was found about a block from the scene of the shooting, on South Main Street. "We think it's the gun," Chief Huston said, reporting it would be turned over to the Federal Bureau of Investigation.

Dr. King was shot while he leaned over a second-floor railing outside his room at the Lorraine Motel. He was chatting with two friends just before starting for dinner.

One of the friends was a musician, and Dr. King had just asked him to play a Negro spiritual, "Precious Lord, Take My Hand," at a rally that was to have been held two hours later in support of striking Memphis sanitationmen.

Paul Hess, assistant administrator at St. Joseph's Hospital, where Dr. King died despite emergency surgery, said the minister had "received a gunshot wound on the right side of the neck, at the root of the neck, a gaping wound."

"He was pronounced dead at 7:05 P.M. Central standard time (8:05 New York time) by staff doctors," Mr. Hess said. "They did everything humanly possible."

Dr. King's mourning associates sought to calm the people they met by recalling his messages of peace, but there was widespread concern by law enforcement officers here and elsewhere over potential reactions.

In a television broadcast after the curfew was ordered here, Mr. Holloman said, "rioting has broken out in parts of the city" and "looting is rampant."

Dr. King had come back to Memphis Wednesday morning to organize support once again for 1,300 sanitation workers who have been striking since Lincoln's Birthday. Just a week ago yesterday he led a march in the strikers' cause that ended in violence. A 16-year-old Negro was killed, 62 persons were injured, and 200 were arrested.

Yesterday, Dr. King had been in his second-floor room—number 306—throughout the day. Just about 6 P.M. he emerged wearing a silkish-looking black suit and white shirt.

Solomon Jones Jr., his driver, had been waiting to take him by car to the home of the Rev. Samual Kyles of Memphis for dinner. Mr. Jones said later he had observed, "It's cold outside; put your topcoat on," and Dr. King replied, "O.K., I will."

TWO MEN IN COURTYARD
Dr. King, an open-faced, genial man, leaned over a green iron railing to chat with an associate, Jesse Jackson, standing just below him in a courtyard parking lot.

"Do you know Ben?" Mr. Jackson asked, introducing Ben Branch of Chicago, a musician who was to play at the night's rally.

"Yes, that's my man!" Dr. King glowed.

The two men recalled Dr. King's asking for the playing of the spiritual. "I really want you to play that tonight," Dr. King said, enthusiastically.

The Rev. Ralph W. Abernathy, perhaps Dr. King's closest friend, was just about to come out of the motel room when the sudden loud noise burst out.

Dr. King toppled to the concrete second-floor walkway. Blood gushed from the right jaw and neck area. His necktie had been ripped off by the blast.

"He had just bent over," Mr. Jackson recalled later. "If he had been standing up, he wouldn't have been hit in the face."

POLICEMEN "ALL OVER"

"When I turned around," Mr. Jackson went on, bitterly, "I saw police coming from everywhere. They said, 'where did it come from?' And I said, 'behind you.' The police were coming from where the shot came."

Mr. Branch asserted that the shot had come from "the hill on the other side of the street."

"When I looked up, the police and the sheriff's deputies were running all around," Mr. Branch declared.

"We didn't need to call the police," Mr. Jackson said. "They were here all over the place."

Mr. Kynes said Dr. King had stood in the open "about three minutes."

Mr. Jones, the driver, said that a squad car with four policemen in it drove down the street only moments before the gunshot. The police had been circulating throughout the motel area on precautionary patrols.

After the shot, Mr. Jones said, he saw a man "with something white on his face" creep away from a thicket across the street.

Someone rushed up with a towel to stem the flow of Dr. King's blood. Mr. Kynes said he put a blanket over Dr. King, but "I knew he was gone." He ran down the stairs and tried to telephone from the motel office for an ambulance.

Mr. Abernathy hurried up with a second larger towel.

POLICE WITH HELMETS

Policemen were pouring into the motel area, carrying rifles and shotguns and wearing riot helmets.

But the King aides said it seemed to be 10 or 15 minutes before a Fire Department ambulance arrived.

Dr. King was apparently still living when he reached the St. Joseph's Hospital operating room for emergency surgery. He was borne in on a stretcher, the bloody towel over his head.

It was the same emergency room to which James H. Meredith, first Negro enrolled at the University of Mississippi, was taken after he was ambushed and shot in June, 1965, at Hernando Miss., a few miles south of Memphis. Mr. Meredith was not seriously hurt.

Outside the emergency room, some of Dr. King's aides waited in forlorn hope. One was Chancey Eskridge, his legal adviser. He broke into sobs when Dr. King's death was announced.

"A man full of like, full of love, and he was shot," Mr. Eskridge said. "He had always lived with that expectation—but nobody ever expected it to happen."

But the Rev. Andrew Young, executive director of Dr. King's Southern Christian Leadership Conference, recalled there had been some talk Wednesday night about possible harm to Dr. King in Memphis.

Mr. Young recalled: "He said he had reached the pinnacle of fulfillment with his nonviolent movement, and these reports did not bother him."

Mr. Young believed that the fatal shot might have been fired from a passing car. "It sounded like a firecracker," he said.

"In a nearby building, a newsman who had been watching a television program thought, however, that "it was a tremendous blast that sounded like a bomb."

There were perhaps 15 persons in the motel courtyard area when Dr. King was shot, all believed to be Negroes and Dr. King's associates.

Past the courtyard is a small empty swimming pool. Then comes Mulberry Street, a short street only three blocks away from storied Beale Street on the fringe of downtown Memphis.

FIRE STATION NEARBY

On the other side of the street is a six-foot brick retaining wall, with bushes and grass atop it and a hillside going on to a patch of trees. Behind the trees is a rusty wire fence enclosing backyards of two-story brick and frame houses.

At the corner at Butler Street is a newish-looking white brick fire station.

Police were reported to have chased a late-model blue or white car through Memphis and north to Millington. A civilian in another car that had a citizens band radio was also reported to have pursued the fleeing car and to have opened fire on it.

The police first cordoned off an area of about five blocks around the Lorraine Motel, chosen by Dr. King for his stay here because it is Negro-owned. The two-story motel is an addition to a small two-story hotel in a largely Negro area.

Mayor Henry Loeb had ordered a curfew here after last week's disorder, and National Guard units had been on duty for five days until they were deactivated Wednesday.

Last night the Mayor reinstated the curfew at 6:35 and declared:

"After the tragedy which has happened in Memphis tonight, for the protection of all our citizens, we are putting the curfew back into effect. All movement is restricted except for health or emergency reasons."

Governor Ellington, calling out the National Guard and pledging all necessary action by the state to prevent disorder, announced:

"For the second time in recent days, I must earnestly ask the people of Memphis and Shelby County to remain calm. I do so again tonight in the face of this most regrettable incident.

"Every possible action is being taken to apprehend the person or persons responsible for committing this act.

"We are also taking precautionary steps to prevent any acts of disorder. I can fully appreciate the feelings and emotions which this crime has aroused, but for the benefit of everyone, all of our citizens must exercise restraint, caution, and good judgment."

National Guard planes flew over the state to bring in contingents of riot-trained highway patrolmen. Units of the Arkansas State Patrol were deputized and brought into Memphis.

Assistant Chief Bartholomew early this morning said that unidentified persons had shot from rooftops and windows at policemen eight or ten times. He said bullets had shattered one police car's windshield, wounding two policemen with flying glass. They were treated at the same hospital were Dr. King died.

Sixty arrests were made for looting, burglary, and disorderly conduct, chief Bartholomew said.

Numerous minor injuries were reported in four hours of clashes between civilians and law enforcement officers. But any serious disorders were under control by 11:15 P.M., Chief Bartholomew said. Early this morning streets were virtually empty except for patrol cars riding without headlights on.

ONCE STABBED IN HARLEM
In his career Dr. King had suffered beatings and blows. Once—on Sept. 20, 1958—he was stabbed in a Harlem department store in New York by a Negro woman later adjudged insane.

That time he underwent a four-hour operation to remove a steel letter opener that had been plunged into his upper left chest. For a time he was on the critical list, but he told his wife, while in the hospital, "I don't hold any bitterness toward this woman."

In Memphis, Dr. King's chief associates met in his room after he died. They include Mr. Young, Mr. Abernathy, Mr. Jackson, the Rev. James Bevel and Hosea Williams.

They had to step across a drying pool of Dr. King's blood to enter. Someone had thrown a crumpled pack of cigarettes into the blood.

After 15 minutes they emerged. Mr. Jackson looked at the blood. He embraced Mr. Abernathy.

"Stand tall!" somebody exhorted.

"Murder! Murder!" Mr. Bevel groaned. "Doc said that's not the way."

"Doc" was what they often called Dr. King.

Then the murdered leader's aides said they would go on to the hall where tonight's rally was to have been held. They wanted to urge calm upon the mourners.

Some policemen sought to dissuade them.

But eventually the group did start out, with a police escort.

At the Federal Bureau of Investigation office here, Robert Jensen, special agent in charge, said the F.B.I. had entered the murder investigation at the request of Attorney General Ramsey Clark.

Last night Dr. King's body was taken to the Shelby County Morgue, according to the police. They said it would be up to Dr. Derry Francisco, county medical examiner, to order further disposition.

300 PROTESTING COLUMBIA STUDENTS BARRICADE OFFICE OF COLLEGE DEAN
By David Bird

NEW YORK, April 24—Three hundred chanting students barricaded the Dean of Columbia College in his office yesterday to protest the construction of a gymnasium in Morningside Park and a defense-oriented program participated in by Columbia University. The protest against the gymnasium extended at one time to the building site, where students tore down a section of fence before being driven off by 30 policemen. The students say that construction of the gymnasium would be "racist" because it would deprive Negroes in the area of recreational facilities. The charge against the defense program, the Institute for Defense Analysis, was that it supported the war effort in Vietnam. The protest, organized by the leftist Students for a Democratic Society, had the support of the other Columbia campus groups. Representatives of several Negro organizations unrelated to Columbia joined the protest. Among the groups were the Harlem chapter of the Congress of Racial Equality, the Harlem Committee for Self-Defense, the United Black Front, and the New York chapter of the Student Nonviolent Coordinating Committee, which is headed nationally by H. Rap Brown. The protest began shortly after noon when about 500 students gathered around the sundial in front of Low Memorial Library, Columbia University's main administrative building. From the sundial, the demonstrators surged up the steps toward the Low building to take their protest directly to the administration.

The Low building was closed, however, and the demonstrators were turned back by university security guards. Behind the guards stood about 150 members of a counter-demonstrations group, the conservative-oriented Students for a Free Campus.

The S.D.S.-led students gathered around Mark Rudd, Columbia's S.D.S. president, who read a letter from David B. Truman, vice president of the university, offering to meet with the group immediately in the McMillan Theater, on the Columbia campus.

The boisterous group shouted down the offer. The students then marched to the site of the new gymnasium, at 113th Street and Morningside Drive, where they tore down a section of chain link fence around the area being cleared for the $11.6-million gymnasium. The police moved in, wielding billy clubs, and arrested one student, Fred Wilson.

The protesters marched four blocks back to the university campus, where Mr. Rudd again addressed the group at the sun-dial. "We're going to have to take a hostage and make them let go of I.D.A. and let go of the gym," he shouted.

With that, Mr. Rudd led the group to Hamilton Hall, the administrative building for Columbia College, the undergraduate arm of the university.

1968

A PROTEST "FOREVER"

At Hamilton Hall, Mr. Rudd took a stand in front of acting Dean Henry S . Coleman's office. He said Mr. Coleman had been selected as the group's hostage.

Mr. Coleman, formerly director of admissions at Columbia, became acting dean in June 1967, when Mr. Truman, then dean of Columbia College, was named vice president and provost of the university.

Mr. Rudd urged the group to remain in Hamilton Hall and outside Mr. Coleman's office until its demands were met, and vowed that the group would stay there "forever" if necessary.

Dean Coleman was not in his office at the time. He appeared a few minutes later, elbowing his way through the crowd, and stood next to Mr. Rudd at the door of his office. Mr. Rudd asked the crowd: "Is this a demonstration?" and the crowd boomed back, "Yes!"

The university recently instituted a rule banning any demonstrations in buildings on the campus, and so the question and answer were obviously meant to point up the group's defiance of the rule.

"Are we going to stay here until our demands are met?" Mr. Rudd asked, and again there was a booming "yes" from his followers. The demonstrators then chanted,

for several minutes, "Hell no, we won't go,"

Dean Coleman, who stood and listened to the chanting, finally said, "I have no control over the demands you are making, but I have no intentions of meeting any demands under a situation such as this."

A voice from the crowd shouted "get on the phone." Dean Coleman replied, "I have no intention of calling the president or vice president of the university under conditions such as this."

The group started singing "We shall not be moved." Leaders of the protest urged the demonstrators to remain in the hall outside Dean Coleman's office, and they promised that food and drink were on the way. Dean Coleman turned and entered his office.

Soon boxes containing soft drinks, carrots, bananas, cake and oranges were brought in.

After the demonstrators had been outside his office for more than an hour, Dean Coleman came out and said, "I repeat, I have no control over your demands."

The demonstration was spearheaded by an informal steering committee established at 2 P.M. by representatives of the Society of Afro-American Students, the Students for a Democratic Society and the Columbia Citizenship council, a group that does tuto-

rial work in the neighborhoods surrounding Columbia.

In addition to demanding that Columbia end construction of the Morningside Park gymnasium and sever its links with the Institute of Defense Analysis, the steering committee also called upon the university to:

• *Terminate all disciplinary actions pending against students as a result of previous demonstrations against the gym and grant a general amnesty to all participants in the current protest.*
• *Lift the ban on campus demonstrations.*
• *Resolve all future disciplinary action against students at open hearings before students and faculty members.*
• *Use its good offices to obtain dismissals of charges against those who participated in demonstrations at the gymnasium site in the past.*

Six students are on probation at Columbia as a result of their participation in protests at the gymnasium site and several persons, including the Rev. A. Kendall Smith, have been arrested.

Dean Coleman, after reviewing the demands, told the student that Mr. Truman had seen the demands and was willing to meet in Wollman Auditorium "now." A steering committee of the protesters met briefly and turned down the offer of the meeting unless they received a written guarantee of amnesty for the protesters.

Mr. Truman later, in an interview in his office in Low Library, said the answer to the amnesty demand was "no." He said he was prepared to have the demonstrators remain in Hamilton Hall "until they get tired."

Once the students had taken over Hamilton Hall, no campus security guards were in evidence and there were no city police anywhere on the campus. By the early morning, the number of demonstrators had grown to about 400.

Shortly after the blockade of the dean's office began, red crepe and posters bearing likenesses of Lenin, Ernest Che Guevara and Malcolm X, the black nationalist who was assassinated in Harlem, were pasted on the walls.

A group of eight Negro youths stood guard outside Dean Coleman's office. At about 10 P.M., a group of Columbia students scuffled briefly with the guards.

One student showed a copy of a leaflet that he said was being distributed in Harlem. It said: "Stop Columbia from taking over Harlem. Black students at Columbia are holding a dean captive and have taken control of the administration building . . . Go to Columbia and help the black students NOW . . ."

At 11:15 P.M., Dean Coleman said he intended to stay in his office "throughout the night if necessary." He refused any other comment.

There were at least two other Columbia faculty members who remained in the dean's office.

Outside the office, Omar Ahmed, an organizer for the United Black Front, said: "We have been running a long campaign against Columbia. This is part of the continuing attack. This is going to be a very hot summer for Columbia University."

Mr. Ahmed said his group intended to "keep up the pressure on the gym, on Harlem Hospital and on Delano Village, which Columbia University bought."

Delano Village is a Harlem housing development bought by Columbia to house staff members of Harlem Hospital, which is affiliated with Columbia. Black organizations charge Columbia has evicted Negroes to make room for hospital personnel. The organizations also blame Columbia for allegedly poor conditions at Harlem Hospital.

The Student Nonviolent Coordinating Committee, one of the most militant black organizations in the country, urged "all people who understand the urgency of this struggle to support the students, community people and their allies."

"It should be crystal clear that the issue at stake is the control by local people of their community and the institutions within their community, and the right of black people to protest injustices perpetrated upon them by institutions such as Columbia University," S.N.C.C. said.

The group's spokesman said that I.D.A. "works on military projects aimed at the oppression of the people of Vietnam" and "develops riot equipment to commit mass genocide against black people here in the U.S."

GROUPS INVITED
William Sales, a 25-year-old Columbia graduate student who is working on a doctorate in international affairs and who is a member of the five-man steering committee leading the protest, said all off-campus groups participating in the demonstration had been invited by the steering committee, which is composed entirely of students.

While the demonstrators filled the corridors of Hamilton Hall, some playing guitars and others sharing blankets and engaging in discussions, Mr. Sales summarized his feeling about Columbia's relations with its neighboring black community.

"They're trying," he said, "to Bogart Harlem," explaining

that he meant act toward Harlem like Humphrey Bogart, the late movie star.

Shortly after 1 A.M., about 50 counterdemonstrators gathered around a statue of Alexander Hamilton about 20 feet from the besieged building and sang choruses of "The Ballad of the Green Berets," a song extolling the heroism of Special Forces troops fighting in Vietnam.

Fred Wilson, the 19-year-old student arrested at the gymnasium site, was charge with assault, criminal mischief, and resisting arrest. He was said to have knocked down three policemen when they tried to stop him from pulling down the fence.

Plans for the construction of the gymnasium have been troubling neighbors of the Negro community as well as some city officials and Columbia alumni. The building is to be erected on a steep rocky slope in Morningside Park, which separates Columbia, on Morningside Heights, from Harlem.

The university signed a 100-year lease with the city for the site in 1961, with rent set at $3,000 a year. The arrangement provided that Columbia build a separate gymnasium and swimming pool for the Harlem community.

Columbia's relations with its neighbors in Harlem have been strained for several years.

One of the problems has been Columbia's expansion, which has resulted in the university's acquisition of more than 100 buildings in the last few years and the eviction of many longtime residents of low-cost rent-controlled housing.

Concerned about crime in its area, Columbia bought many hotels that were well-known havens for prostitutes and narcotics addicts and attempted to evict these tenants, but some community groups objected, saying Columbia should have undertaken the rehabilitation rather than the eviction of the residents.

Recently, when Columbia began attempts to rehabilitate some of its tenants, the efforts were denounced in leaflets.

HUNDREDS ARE HURT IN CLASHES IN PARIS
By Lloyd Garrison

PARIS, Saturday, May 25—A student demonstration that started peacefully yesterday evening turned into the most violent and widespread battles with the police since the student revolt began more than two weeks ago.

For the first time, the fighting overflowed to the Right Bank.

One group of students penetrated as far as the Bourse, the Paris stock exchange, and set fires inside and in front of the building.

Late last night, the Government radio appealed for all available doctors to assemble at the Sorbonne medical school, where an emergency hospital was set up to care for casualties on both sides.

Hundreds of wounded policemen and students were carried away by medical students and interns in makeshift ambulances.

RIOTS FOLLOWED SPEECH
The fighting began 30 minutes after President de Gaulle had finished his radio and television appeal for a return to calmness. The first clashes erupted on the Rue de Lyon, where the police had blocked well over 20,000 marchers from entering the Place de la Bastille. Most of the demonstrators were students, but some were workers and some had started as bystanders.

Barred from the Place de la Bastille by the police, the students erected barricades with felled trees, paving stones, and garbage cans overflowing with refuse.

After standing face to face with the forefront of the student column for more than an hour, the police finally charged at 9:46 P.M., using tear gas and concussion grenades. The huge crowd fought from one barricade to another, slowly retreating

10 blocks to the Gare de Lyon, setting fire to the barricades as it withdrew.

Within an hour, the fighting had spread over a two-square-mile area in the old Marias district and had also spilled over the Left Bank into the Latin Quarter.

RETURNED TO LEFT BANK

About 300 students tried to occupy the Bourse, on the Rue du 4 Septembre, in the heart of the business district. They set fires inside the building, pulled down quotation boards and broke the great windows surrounding the grand hall before they were driven out.

By 11 P.M., more than 30 hit-and-run battles were raging in widely scattered parts of the city, from the Place de la Republique and the Opéra on the Right Bank to the Luxembourg Gardens and the Place Maubert on the Left Bank.

By midnight, most of the students had barricades in the Latin Quarter. Many of the barricades were built out of burned-out cars and trucks left in the streets after Thursday night's rioting.

There was a temporary lull in the fighting on the Boulevard Saint-Michel near the Luxembourg Gardens when Red Cross workers and medical students formed a cordon between the students and the police. But the police charged the barricades from a side street. Nurses wept when the fighting was renewed.

STUDENTS CROSS SEINE

The running battles with policemen marked the first time that student violence had flared up on the right bank of the Seine. Ever since the American and North Vietnamese began their talks here two weeks ago, the police had barred student demonstrators from crossing the bridges over the Seine from the Latin Quarter. But yesterday the students were authorized to assemble in front of the Gare de Lyon, about two blocks from the Austerlitz Bridge.

The police assumed that the students were going to demonstrate in front of the railroad station and then disperse. Instead, the students marched on the Bastille, traditional staging ground for left-wing demonstrations.

It was the fifth major battle between students and policemen since rioting broke out at the Sorbonne May 10.

The students were in a fighting mood after the Government's decision earlier this week to forbid the return to France of Daniel Cohn-Bendit, the French-born West German student at the nearby University of Nanterre, where the New Left student movement was spawned.

ENTRY IS REFUSED

Mr. Cohn-Bendit, who was in Frankfurt Thursday for a student meeting, was refused entry to France yesterday when he tried to cross the border at Strasbourg.

In the eyes of many observers, the decision to cordon off the Place de la Bastille made it almost physically impossible for the student column—which was more than half a mile long—to reverse itself on the relatively narrow Rue de Lyon.

The following exchange took place between Jacques Sauvageot, leader of the National Students' Union, and a police inspector whose forces blocked the Place de la Bastille.

Mr. Sauvageot: "Just let us into the square and then we'll disperse. There are at least nine streets leading out of the square, and dispersing will be easy."

Inspector: "My orders are to block you here. You can demonstrate all you want in front of the Gare de Lyon, but not here."

Mr. Sauvageot: "But how in the world do you expect us to turn around? The tail of the column hasn't even passed the Gare. We can't even communicate with it."

Inspector: "That's your problem, not mine."

FLAG THROWN DOWN

At the Gare de Lyon, which is Paris's largest railroad station, a small, swarthy man in a bright red sweater shinned up a flagpole, tore down the flag of France, and threw it into the gutter. Thousands of voices cheered, then joined to sing "The Internationale."

A hush fell as the man began to hoist himself up the flagpole again. He reached the top and attached the red flag to the staff. The crowd cheered again.

"Something has happened in France today, she has found her spirit again, we are French again," said a woman standing nearby. She would not give her name. "Today, I am a Frenchwoman—that's all and that's enough," she said.

Many students and workers went into battle wearing motorcycle helmets and armed with garbage can lids for shields.

No quarter was given by either side. Demonstrators and unlucky bystanders were surrounded by squads of angry policemen and often beaten for as long as five minutes before being dumped, limp and unconscious, into ambulances. Student stretcher-bearers with Red Cross armbands and white surgeon's smocks often braved the crossfire of rocks and tear gas grenades to pick up casualties.

The workers were also on the march in two huge columns on both sides of the river.

About 60,000 marched from the Bastille to the Place de la République and along the Grands Boulevards to the Opéra.

About 50,000 others start-

ed from Place Balard, in the southwestern part of Paris, and marched to the Austerlitz station.

A group of rioters sacked a police records office near City Hall, on the Right Bank, this morning. They broke up furniture and were burning the files when police reinforcements arrived. The rioters then fled.

Early this morning, the Interior Minister, Christian Fouchet, issued a statement attributing the riots to three elements—students who had lost their sense of reason, petty criminals who fought with "murderous stupidity," and "anarchists trained in guerrilla tactics."

Mr. Fouchet praised the restraint of the police and said it was remarkable in the circumstances that no one had been killed in Paris. He called on the city's people to "vomit out this hooligan element."

KENNEDY SHOT AND GRAVELY WOUNDED AFTER WINNING CALIFORNIA PRIMARY; SUSPECT SEIZED IN LOS ANGELES HOTEL
By Warren Weaver Jr.

LOS ANGELES, Wednesday, June 5—Senator Robert F. Kennedy was shot and critically wounded by an unidentified gunman this

morning just after he made his victory speech in the California primary election.

Moments after the shots were fired, the New York Senator lay on the cement floor of a kitchen corridor outside the ballroom of the Ambassador Hotel while crowds of screaming and wailing supporters crowded around him.

On his arrival at Good Samaritan Hospital a spokesman described Senator Kennedy's condition as "stable." He was described as breathing but not apparently conscious.

Frank Mankiewicz, Senator Kennedy's press aide, was quoted as saying, at 4:15 A.M.: "He is breathing well and has good heart. I would not expect he is conscious."

SHOT TWICE IN HEAD
Mr. Mankiewicz said the Senator had been shot twice in the head—once in the forehead and once near the right ear. He was transferred to Good Samaritan Hospital after a brief stop at General Receiving Hospital.

The Rev. Thomas Peacha said he had administered the last rites of the Roman Catholic Church in the hospital's emergency room. This is normal procedure when a Catholic has been possibly seriously injured.

The suspected assailant, a short, dark-haired youth wearing blue denims, was immediately seized by a group of Kennedy supporters, including the huge Negro professional football player Roosevelt Grier. They pinned the assailant's arms to a stainless steel counter, the gun still in his hand.

WIFE BY HIS SIDE

Senator Kennedy lay on the floor, blood running from his back. His right eye was open but the other was partly closed as his wife, Ethel, kneeled at his side. His shirt was pulled open, and a rosary could be seen on his chest.

Richard Tuck, a Kennedy aide who was at his side at the time of the shooting, said the Senator's condition was "very bad." Within minutes he was rushed to a hospital.

Some witnesses reported that he had been shot in the back of the head or neck. Others indicated that at least one bullet had entered his torso.

A physician who gave Senator Kennedy emergency treatment before he was removed from the hotel said that his pulse was 130 but "full and bounding" and that the heart beat was good. The Senator was not conscious. He was given oxygen and intravenous plasma.

Dr. George Lambert, a physician with American Airlines, was in the hotel and responded to the call for a doctor. Several doctors responded. Mr. Lambert said that he had not treated Senator Kennedy but that he had treated two others who had been shot. He said one was a man shot in the left side and the other a man shot in the leg, both apparently bystanders. He said they were not seriously wounded and were taken to the same hospital as the Senator.

Senator Kennedy's brother, President John F. Kennedy, was killed by Lee Harvey Oswald in Dallas on Nov. 22, 1963.

It was only moments after the Senator had concluded a brief victory statement to several hundred cheering supporters when the incident occurred. He was being escorted out a back door of the ballroom, behind the rostrum, and through the kitchen corridor to an adjoining room that was serving temporarily as a working press room.

Mr. Kennedy had been scheduled to hold a post-election news conference there.

STOOD BY TABLE

When four or five shots rang out, reporters and photographers rushed from the press room while other persons from the ballroom audience crowded in from the other side of the hall.

Karl Uecker, assistant maitre d'hotel at the Ambassador, said he was walking in front of Senator and Mrs. Kennedy when the gunman began shooting.

"I'm right in front of him," Mr. Uecker said 15 minutes after the shooting. "There were three shots, one after the other.

"I recognized the danger and I grabbed him by the neck."

He was describing his capture of the gunman.

Mr. Uecker said the gunman had been standing by the corner of a work table in the kitchen passageway and that "he looked like a houseman."

Mr. Uecker said he was aware that Senator Kennedy had collapsed to the floor behind him.

"The first or second shot hit him," Mr. Uecker said.

The suspect said nothing when the maitre d' grappled with him.

"I wrestled with the gunman," Mr. Uecker said.

He looked over the heads of the reporters interviewing him and said: "I thought it was a joke or something. It sounded like Chinese firecrackers or something. I had my hand on Kennedy, I was leading him, and his wife was on my other hand."

The Senator's assailant was a youthful man with an olive complexion. He had a stocky build and dark curly hair.

HELD ON COUNTER

Moments after the shooting he was lifted by Mr. Grier and other persons to the serving counter top and held prone.

All the while frenzied adherents of Mr. Kennedy were screaming oaths at the gunman.

"You bastard, you'll fry for this," one slight, dark man shouted as he jumped up and down on the serving counter.

When the police arrived, they carried the gunman horizontally, four or five of them holding his arms and legs, through the press room and out into the hotel lobby.

Among those who seized the man was William Barry, a bank vice president from New York who has been serving as Senator Kennedy's chief security aide during his primary campaigns.

A half hour after the shooting, the Los Angeles police reported that two suspects had been arrested and that the Ambassador has been surrounded by police. The latter report indicated a suspicion that other men might have been involved in the shooting.

Just after the Senator fell wounded and bleeding, Mrs. Kennedy rose from his side to warn away photographers, reporters and others in the horrified crowd who were pushing in.

"Get back, get back," she shouted, her tanned face drawn. Then, as space opened in the corridor, she returned to kneel beside her husband, who was breathing deeply.

Amid the curses, a voice from the crowd shouted: "Someone pray!" At that, Mr. Kennedy took his rosary beads and tightened his hand about them.

The ambulance carried the senator to Central Receiving Hospital. Then he was taken to Good Samaritan Hospital in an ambulance with Mrs. Kennedy. His head was bandaged and there appeared to be plasma in use.

Pierre Salinger, Mr. Kennedy's aide, said at Central Receiving Hospital that the wounds were serious. Mr. Salinger said Mr. Kennedy had been shot in the head and in the body.

Earl Williman, a Kennedy supporter who had been standing near the Senator at the time of the gunfire, said Mr. Kennedy had been shot near the ear.

"All I could see," Mr. Williman said, "was the man here in the kitchen. He stepped up and shot the Senator right near the ear. I didn't see any more. I hit the man and several of us held him."

Mr. Kennedy had just won a major victory in his campaign for the Democratic Presidential nomination. His short victory speech, full of quiet jokes about his dog and his family, closed with these words: "On to Chicago and let's win there."

CZECHOSLOVAKIA INVADED BY RUSSIANS AND FOUR OTHER WARSAW PACT FORCES
By Tad Szulc

PRAGUE, Wednesday, Aug. 21— Czechoslovakia was occupied early today by troops of the Soviet Union and four of its Warsaw Pact allies in a series of swift land and air movements.

Airborne Soviet troops and paratroopers surrounded the building of the Communist Party Central Committee, along with five tanks. At least 25 tanks were seen in the city.

Several persons were reported killed early this morning. Unconfirmed reports said that two Czechoslovak soldiers and a woman were killed by Bulgarian tank fire in front of the Prague radio building shortly before the station was captured and went off the air.

[Soviet troops began shooting at Czechoslovak demonstrators outside the Prague radio building at 7:25 A.M., Reuters reported. C.T.K., the Czechoslovak press agency was quoted by United Press International as having said that citizens were throwing themselves in front of the tanks in an attempt to block the seizure of the city.]

MOVE A SURPRISE

The Soviet move caught Czechoslovaks by surprise, although all day yesterday there were indications of new tensions.

Confusion was caused in the capital by leaflets dropped from unidentified aircraft asserting that Antonin Novotny, the President of Czechoslovakia who was deposed in March by the Communist liberals, had been pushed out by a "clique."

The leaflets said that Mr. Novotny remained the country's legal President.

At 5 A.M. the Prague radio, still in the hands of adherents of the Communist liberals, broadcast a dramatic appeal to the population in the name of Alexander Dubček, the party First Secretary, to go to work as usual this morning.

The radio station said: "These may be the last reports you will hear because the technical facilities in our hands are insufficient."

The announcer said that Czechoslovakia must heed the orders of the Presidium of the Central Committee, "which is in continuing session even though the building is surrounded by foreign units."

The radio said that it remained loyal to President Ludvik Svoboda and Mr. Dubček.

While earlier this morning the radio appealed to the population not to resist invading troops from the Soviet Union, Poland, East Germany, Hungary, and Bulgaria, small-arms fire was heard shortly after 5 A.M. in the Maala Strana district of Prague.

At 2:45 A.M., as part of this dispatch was being filed by telex, the city appeared calm, though the roar of aircraft and the broadcast, heard by many, had awakened the population.

Starting shortly after midnight a veritable airlift of Soviet and other Warsaw Pact aircraft flew troops into Prague. Ruzine Airport had been secured earlier by Czechoslovak troops though it was not known under whose command they were operating.

At 5:15 A.M. aircraft were still heard landing and taking off.

Despite the Prague radio broadcasts, the whereabouts of Mr. Dubček, Mr. Svoboda, and their associates was not known.

In any event, the invasion that began at 11 o'clock last night when the Czechoslovak border was crossed from several sides evidently put an end to the Dubček experiment in democracy under Communism that was initiated in January.

The expectation was that the occupying forces would sponsor the establishment of a new regime that would be more amenable to orthodox Communist views of Moscow and its partners.

There are about 5,000 United States citizens in Czechoslovakia at this time, of whom about 1,500 are tourists and 400 are delegates to an international geological congress.

Shirley Temple Black, the former actress, is among the Americans at the Hotel Alcron here.

The news broadcast early today said that Soviet troops had sealed all border exits in Austria. Trains were not running and airline operations were halted.

After 3 A.M., all city lights went out.

APPEAL TO PUBLIC

A broadcast at 1:30 A.M. had appealed to the population not to resist the advance and for officials to remain at their jobs.

Yesterday, as the tension mounted, the Czechoslovak leadership was reported to have been seriously concerned over renewed Soviet press attacks on Mr. Dubček's liberalization program.

Last night the party Presidium met unexpectedly under Mr. Dubček's chairmanship, presumably to discuss the new tensions.

At a confidential meeting Saturday with five progressive

members of the Presidium, Czechoslovak editors were told that a successful party congress next month was the most urgent priority in the country and that, therefore, their cooperation was needed.

INTERNAL BATTLE CONTINUES

Internally, however, the political tug of war between the progressives and the conservatives continued.

Rude Pravo, the party's official organ, whose editor Oldrich Svestka, is regarded as a leading conservative, published three articles today critical of the progressives' policies.

Another example of mounting political sensitiveness was an announcement by the Foreign Ministry, published in *Rude Pravo* and later distributed by the official press agency, that Henry Kamm, a correspondent of *The New York Times*, "will not be allowed to return to Czechoslovakia."

Mr. Kamm, who left Prague for the United States and a vacation Saturday, was charged by *Rude Pravo* with "slanderous information" and "fabrications" concerning its editorial staff.

Dispatches by Mr. Kamm published in *The Times* on Aug. 14 and 15 described a continuing struggle between Mr. Svetska and the progressive members of the staff. One dispatch said that Mr. Svetska, who is a member of the party's Presidium, had curtailed coverage of the visit here earlier this month by President Tito of Yugoslavia, who is a backer of the Dubček faction.

The newspaper said yesterday that "the management of *Rude Pravo* resolutely opposes this shameless provocation, which had become the pretext for a slanderous press campaign against *Rude Pravo* abroad," and that "it is indubitable that its aim is the unconcealed effort to interfere with our internal affairs."

Mr. Svetska, however, came under attack himself in the liberal weekly *Reporter*, which in its current issue reported that he had played down the Tito visit. The magazine said that Mr. Svetska "has set up a sort of internal police which watches over everything that goes into print."

Rude Pravo's counterattack yesterday included the front page article signed by Mr. Svetska, in effect defending the conservative position. He wrote that unless the Communist party regained its "antibureaucratic" character and returned to the aims of the workers, the new "demagogic slogans" could turn against the party itself.

In an allusion to the progressives' efforts to oust conservatives from the key jobs, Mr. Svetska wrote that democracy was not served "by making life miserable for the honest officials and members who have not discredited themselves, by turning them away from political activity."

A second article took to task the television commentator, Jiri Kanturek, for what it said were attempts to discredit Mr. Svetska.

A third article charged that a "secret committee" had been established to attack the people's militia, a paramilitary organization widely considered to be controlled by the conservatives. The article referred critically to the signing of petitions in Prague last week for the abolition of the militia.

THOUSANDS MARCH
By J. Anthony Lukas

CHICAGO, Friday, Aug. 30— More than 150 people, including nine convention delegates, were arrested last night after National Guardsmen halted 3,000 persons marching toward the International Amphitheatre.

The guardsmen then fired tear gas to disperse the rest of the crowd. Later they fired more tear gas into ranks of demonstrators in front of the Conrad Hilton Hotel.

The first canisters of gas arched into crowds on Michigan Avenue at exactly 10:30 P.M., just as Vice President Humphrey was mounting the podium in the Amphitheatre to make his acceptance speech.

The arrests occurred at 18th Street and Michigan Avenue after the mass march, led by Dick Gregory, the comedian and black militant, was halted by guardsmen in armored personnel carriers and jeeps with barbed-wire barriers mounted on their hoods.

ORDERED TO TURN

The guardsmen told the demonstrators that they would have to turn west on 18th Street. Mr. Gregory insisted that all members of the huge throng were invited to his home on East 55th Street, south of the Amphitheatre.

"We have a right to go to my house," Mr. Gregory said.

But Brig. Gen. John R. Phipps, field commander of the National Guard contingent here, refused to let them proceed. High-ranking city officials said that the march was being blocked on the advice of the Secret Service.

The marchers decided to insist on their rights. One by one they walked through the barrier where they were seized by National Guardsmen and escorted to huge police vans.

OTHER DELEGATES

The first marcher through was Mr. Gregory himself, dressed in tan coveralls and a rain hat. Then came Tommy Fraser, a crippled delegate from Oklahoma riding in a wheel chair.

Then came other delegates, including Murray Kempton, the *New York Post* columnist, who is a delegate from Manhattan; Peter Weiss and the Rev. Richard Neuhaus of the Bronx, and Richard Samuel of Westfield, N.J.

Earlier, an enforcement officer had told delegates that if they kept their delegates' cards on they would be escorted to the Amphitheatre about four miles away.

The delegates caucused on the sidewalk and decided to seek arrest instead. They took off their credentials. "We have been told, as delegates, the we cannot go where we are going on our evening stroll," Mr. Neuhuas said. "We will sit here on the pavement," he said, "until the Chicago police are ready to recognize the civil liberties of private citizens."

The delegates sat on the sidewalk briefly, then got up and moved through the barricades where they were arrested.

After 23 persons had been arrested, others in the march insisted that the National Guardsmen arrest them, too.

There was confusion last night about exactly how many persons had been arrested. One police official said 160 persons were taken into custody, but another official put the figure at 423.

Police vans, which held 50 persons, hauled the demonstrators to the central detention facilities at police headquarters. Five special night courts were set up in the building to speed the arraignment procedures, which started at 10 P.M. Arraignment was still going on past midnight.

SOLDIERS FIRE GAS

After the arrests had been made, the guardsmen fired tear gas to clear the area of the demonstrators who were seated on the sidewalk in front of the checkpoint.

The demonstrators, wiping their eyes, poured north along Michigan Avenue and back into Grant Park.

A police helicopter flew low overhead with searchlights sweeping the fleeing crowd.

Demonstrators streamed into medical stations in the area set up this week by the Medical Committee for Human Rights.

Meanwhile, in front of the Hilton, National Guardsmen fired four or five tear gas canisters into a crowd of about 5,000 youths gathered in Grant Park across the street from the hotel.

First aid volunteers passed around pots of water with which the youths tried to clear their eyes. Others dunked their heads in a fountain in the park.

Some of the demonstrators responded by throwing bottles and cans at the Hilton.

There were reports of only a few scattered incidents involving physical contact between demonstrators and security forces. Mercy Hospital in downtown Chicago reported that several youths had been treated early today for head and scalp injuries.

The march led by Mr. Gregory was one of the three marches that moved south from the Loop area during the day in an attempt to reach the Amphitheatre. All three were turned back.

The first march was organized by the Wisconsin delegation to protest police "brutality" in suppressing demonstrations.

Donald O. Peterson, the delegation chairman, said before the march, "I just want to take a walk through the streets of Chicago to see if this is a free and open city and to show we're free men."

Shortly after 4 P.M., the march left the Bismarck Hotel on West Randolph Street, led by Mr. Peterson, with a pink daisy in his hand. He was followed by most of his own delegation and many sympathetic delegates from other states—perhaps 200 persons.

But as the march proceeded down the sidewalk along Randolph Street and turned south on State Street, it picked up thousands of adherents.

One of those who joined was Milton Shapp, a Pennsylvania delegate and former Democratic nominee for Governor, who said, "I saw them walking and I got in. I'd rather walk than ride in Daley's buses."

ENCOUNTER POLICE

The marchers walked a mile and a half down the State Street sidewalk to 16th Street, where they found a solid police line stretching across the street, backed by steel-helmeted National Guardsmen in armored personnel carriers.

Police officers told David Carley, retiring Democratic National Committeeman from Wisconsin, that the procession was a parade and thus required a parade permit. Without a permit, the officers said, the procession would not be allowed to cross 16th Street.

After conferring for a few minutes with police officers, most of the marchers turned around and headed back toward the Loop.

However, about 10 delegates and 40 to 50 others stayed on, insisting on their right to pass through the barriers.

Finally, Richard L. Elrod, an assistant counsel to the city, agreed to let the small group continue on down State Street as far as 39th Street.

They walked down the sidewalk, accompanied by the two

police patrol cars, until they reached 39th Street, where the delegates dropped out of the march. But the other, younger demonstrators continued two blocks south to West Root Street, where they turned right for a block and a half—reaching a point about five blocks from the Amphitheatre.

There they were met by 10 or 12 police cars and three or four vans, which disgorged dozens of policemen. The policemen refused to let the demonstrators pass.

By this time, however, the march had attracted more than 300 Negro youngsters who poured out of the huge housing projects lining the street. The Negroes danced around the demonstrators asking, "What's going on?" and "Where did your people come from?"

About an hour after the march led by the Wisconsin delegates, another march moved off from Grant Park in front of the Conrad Hilton Hotel. Several hundred persons marched south on Michigan Avenue to 16th Street, where they, too, ran into a line of policemen and National Guardsmen.

They turned around and retreated to the park several blocks south of the Hilton where they joined with several thousand other demonstrators.

All three marches took place after a mass rally in the afternoon in the park across from the Hilton Hotel.

At the rally, attended by two to three thousand young persons, leaders of the Mobilization Committee to End the War in Vietnam urged the youths to go back to their communities and create "one, two, three hundred Chicagos."

Tom Hayden, a leader of the mobilization committee, told the huge throng seated on the grass beneath the trees:

"If they want blood to flow from our heads the blood will flow from a lot of other heads around this city and around the country."

"We must take to the streets," he said, "for the streets belong to the people."

The spectators, some of whom waved Vietcong flags and the black flags of anarchism, cheered and shouted over and over again, "The streets belong to the people."

Standing on an upturned trash barrel under a tree and speaking through a sound system whose speakers were held up by eager young hands, Mr. Hayden said, "It may well be that the era of organized, peaceful, and orderly demonstrations is coming to an end and that other methods will be needed."

"We are now beginning to fight because we must, because it has been imposed on us—we are beginning to fight for our own survival. And if we can survive in Chicago we can survive anywhere."

The demonstrators, some of them still wearing bandages from battles earlier this week, cheered and laughed and cheered again.

Rennie Davis, a mobilization committee coordinator, who had been clubbed on the head by the police, clambered atop the trash barrel, his head swathed in white bandages.

"We don't want people to tell us how we must support Hubert Humphrey because he is a little better than Nixon," Mr. Davis said. "Hubert Humphrey and Richard Nixon both represent all that is old, all that is ugly, all that is bigoted, all that is repressive in America today. They must be pushed into the sea."

"Don't vote for Humphrey, don't vote for Nixon," he shouted. "Join us in the streets of America.

"We are going out now all over the country to build a National Liberation Front for America," he said. "The slogan of our front will be 'There can be no peace in the United States until there is peace in Vietnam.'"

Hundreds of steel-helmeted Illinois National Guardsmen armed with M-1 Rifles and carrying tear-gas spray guns on their backs stood elbow to elbow three rows deep along Michigan Avenue in front of Grant Park.

There were no incidents involving the guardsmen or the police who stood across the street in front of the Hilton.

But twice during the afternoon, hostile, middle-aged men traded blows with demonstrators on the edge of the crowd. One red-faced man shouted, "Are you going to let these damned Communists get away with this?" as he punched a young man dressed in Levis and a T-shirt.

An hour later, a man in a neat blue suit and tie shouted "you people are dirty" at a group of youths and then tussled on the grass with a tall man in a sports shirt. Both were led away by the police.

Hundreds of persons gazed out the windows of the Conrad Hilton at the crowd in the park and from time to time demonstrators looked up at the windows, making with their fingers the "V for victory" sign that has become a symbol of the antiwar movement.

AT LEAST 20 DEAD AS MEXICO STRIFE REACHES A PEAK

By Paul Montgomery

MEXICO CITY, Oct. 2—Federal troops fired on a student rally with rifles and machine guns tonight, killing at least 20 people and wounding more than 100.

The troops moved on a rally of 3,000 people in the square of a vast housing project just as night was falling. In an inferno of firing that lasted an hour, the army strafed the area with machine guns mounted on jeeps and tanks.

About 1,000 troops took part in the action. Tanks, armored cars and jeeps followed them, spurting .30- and .50-caliber machine-gun fire.

Buses, trolley cars and other vehicles were set on fire at several places in the city. Ambulances screamed through the rainy night.

Many women and children were among the dead and injured.

GAMES CAST INTO DOUBT

Also injured was Gen. José Hernández Toledo, a paratroop commander who has led troops into university campuses three times over the last two years. He was undergoing surgery tonight for a stomach wound.

According to the army, at least one soldier was killed and 12 were wounded by sniper fire from apartment buildings towering over the square.

The night's events cast into serious question the prospects for the Olympic Games, which are scheduled to begin here on Oct. 12. Until the troops moved in, it seemed that both the Government and the city's rebellious students were working to establish an atmosphere of calm after some 10 weeks of struggling.

In a statement tonight, the Defense Minister, Gen. Marcelino García Barragán, said that the troops had moved on the rally after snipers fired on the Federal District riot police guarding the nearby Foreign Ministry and a vocational school. The general's statement was disputed by many witnesses.

HOSPITAL FULL OF WOUNDED

The army moved immediately to keep reporters from the Red Cross hospital, near the housing project, three miles north of the center of Mexico City. But an intern in the hospital said that it was full of wounded, all of them civilians. Army ambulances took the dead and many other wounded to the Military Hospital, which was closed to reporters.

Witnesses described the widespread killing in the square. Six dead—two of them women— could be counted by this correspondent in a small section of the square.

The clash was the worst in student demonstrations that have been going on in the capital since July 23.

In the last serious fighting, two weeks ago, at least 7 and perhaps 17 people, most of them students, were killed. High-school and university students have been on strike here for two months to protest the incident. In all, 150,000 have stayed away from classes.

The rally tonight took place in the Plaza of the Three Cultures, a paved area 100 yards square, named for its proximity to some Aztec ruins, a colonial church, and the modern Foreign Ministry. On two sides of the square are 12-story apartment buildings of the Nonoalco-Tlatelolco housing project, a 10-year-old middle-class development housing 76,000 people.

On the third side is Vocational School 7, one of the institutions involved in the strike. It has been occupied by riot policemen for 12 days. The fourth side fronts on the ruins, consisting of reconstructed ceremonial platforms and building walls interspersed with grass. The stone for the colonial church was taken from the Aztec buildings, so there is little left but foundations.

The rally had been called by the 200-member National Strike Committee to seek the withdrawal of riot policemen from Vocational School 7 and of federal troops from the Santo Tomás campus of the National Polytechnic Institute, a mile away. The students had planned to march from the rally to Santo Tomás.

By 5 P.M., the rally participants were assembled. Many students shouted their school "locomotive" cheers and passed out leaflets. Parents, children, and a sprinkling of workmen also turned out. Some workmen and peasant groups recently expressed sympathy for the student strike.

"WE ASK YOU TO GO HOME"
The first speaker, a youth in a red sweater, announced that the march to Santo Tomás would not take place. He said there were 22 truckloads of troops, 14 jeeps with machine guns and many tanks at the Polytechnic campus. "The committee does not believe in bloodshed," he said. "We ask you to go home when this meeting is over."

The crowd hooted and hissed mildly but appeared to be in good humor. The speaker's estimate of the troop strength at Santo Tomás was accurate. But, by 5:30 the troops had left the campus and were on the way to the rally site.

Just after 6 P.M., while the rally was going on, shooting broke out near the Foreign Ministry. The army said snipers in a nearby building had started it. Other witnesses blamed the army.

Troops moved from the Foreign Ministry through the Aztec ruins toward the plaza, firing as they ran. The crowd at the rally swirled in panic, running from the advancing force. Snipers, presumably allied with the students, opened up from the buildings all around the plaza.

Throughout the area, people ran for cover. The firing became louder. Grenade bursts and flares exploded over the square. The ground was littered with bodies.

In surrounding buildings, people ran for cover, screaming. Families lay on the floor, away from the windows.

"JUST SHOT EVERYONE"
"They came without warning," said one man who was there. "There was no tear gas. They just shot at everyone."

By 7 P.M., the pitched battle was over, although sporadic firing continued through the night.

An hour after the fighting, troops still crouched behind walls and buildings while pedestrians walked past them unconcerned. Soldiers brought stretcher after stretcher of the dead out of the plaza.

Scores of young men, and even a few children, were led away, their hands behind their heads. And in the midst of it all was a little girl led by her mother. The girl held a towel over her left eye. Blood dripped from under the bandage.

3 MEN FLY AROUND THE MOON ONLY 70 MILES FROM SURFACE
By John Noble Wilford

HOUSTON, Wednesday, Dec. 25—The three astronauts of Apollo 8 yesterday became the first men to orbit the moon. Early today, after flying 10 times around that desolate realm of dream and scientific mystery, they started their return to earth.

They fired the spacecraft's main rocket engine at 1:10 A.M. to kick them out of lunar orbit and to carry them toward a splashdown in the Pacific Ocean on Friday.

Through the static of 231,000 miles, as Apollo 8 swung around from behind the moon and started for earth, one of the astronauts dispelled any doubts, saying, "Please be informed there is a Santa Claus."

57-HOUR RETURN TRIP
It would be a 57-hour return trip from the most far-reaching voyage of the space age thus far—or of

any other previous age. The astronauts had seen, as no other men had, the ancient lunar craters, plains and rugged mountains from as close as 70 miles.

At 4:59 A.M. yesterday, about 20 hours before the return trip, Col. Frank Borman of the Air Force, Capt. James A. Lovell Jr. of the Navy and Maj. William A. Anders of the Air Force, swept into an orbit of the moon by firing the spacecraft's main rocket. This occurred after they flew around the leading edge of the moon and were directly behind the earth's only natural satellite.

"We got it! We've got it!" exclaimed a mission commentator of the National Aeronautics and Space Administration as the spacecraft emerged from the behind the moon 24 minutes later, and was clearly flying a safe and smooth orbit.

BUSINESSLIKE REPORT

The calm and laconic Apollo explorers, however, were all business. Captain Lovell's first message to earth was simply:

"Go ahead, Houston. Apollo 8. Burn complete. Our orbit is 169.1 by 60.5—169.1 by 60.5."

The astronauts flew twice around the moon in the egg-shaped orbit, then dropped to a circular orbit nearly 70 miles above the ancient craters, plains and rugged mountains of the lunar surface.

As they beamed their first live television from orbit on Christmas Eve morning, they described the surface of the moon as a colorless gray, "like dirty beach sand with lots of footprints on it" and said it "looks like plaster of Paris."

At about 9:30 P.M. the astronauts began their second and last television show from lunar orbit. It ran some 30 minutes and showed the bright moon, in a pitch-black sky, outside the spacecraft window.

EARTH LIKE AN "OASIS"

Colonel Borman described the moon as a "vast, lonely and forbidding sight," adding that it was "not a very inviting place to live or work."

Captain Lovell saw the earth as a "grand oasis in the big vastness of space."

Major Anders was most impressed by "the lunar sunrise and sunsets."

As the telecast neared its end, Colonel Borman said "Apollo 8 has a message for you." With that, Major Anders began reading the opening verses from the Book of Genesis about creation of the earth.

"In the beginning," Major Anders read, "God created the heavens and the earth.

"And the earth was without form and voice; and the darkness was upon the face of the deep . . ."

Captain Lovell then took up with the verse beginning, "And God called the light day, and the darkness He called night."

Colonel Borman closed the reading with the verse that read:

"And God called the dry land Earth; and the gathering together of the water called the Seas: and God saw that it was good."

SENDS HOLIDAY GREETINGS

After that Colonel Borman signed off, saying:

"Good-bye, good night. Merry Christmas. God bless all of you, all of you on the good earth."

Glynn S. Lunney, one of the flight directors here, told reporters earlier, "We have a completely 'go' spacecraft."

George M. Low, the spacecraft manager at the Manned Spacecraft Center, said he was "altogether happy" with the mission—the most ambitious and daring thus far in the nation's $24-billion Apollo project to land men on the moon next year.

Although the mission's object was not primarily scientific, Dr. John Dietrich of the space center's geology and geochemistry branch said that the television pictures and astronaut descriptions had "demonstrated their ability to observe from the spacecraft to a degree I think surprised most of us."

The astronauts' color movies and still pictures, expected to be the most spectacular and most valuable of all the pictures, will be brought back for processing and analysis by scientists. Many of the pictures were taken of a site in the Sea of Tranquility where American astronauts may land next year.

The lunar-orbiting mission, the second manned flight of the Apollo project, is expected to be followed by an earth-orbiting flight in February or March to test the lunar landing vehicle. The first landing on the moon could come as early as next June.

Apollo 8's historic voyage round and round the moon came about 69 hours after the spacecraft was launched by a Saturn 5 rocket at Cape Kennedy, Fla., last Saturday morning.

The spacecraft was falling faster and faster toward the moon's vicinity, having crossed from earth's to the moon's sphere of gravitational influence when the astronauts were more than 214,000 miles away from earth.

To make a fine correction of their aim the astronauts fired the spacecraft's small maneuvering rockets. Ground controllers, fearing some of the Apollo computers' navigation data might be incorrect, radioed a new set of numbers into the instrument's memory unit.

Then Maj. Gerald Carr of the Marine Corps, the astronaut acting as capsule communicator in the control room, radioed:

"Apollo 8, you are riding the best bird we can find."

"Thanks a lot, troops," Major Anders replied. "We'll see you on the other side."

At 4:49 A.M. as the spacecraft curved behind the moon, the signals died out. Apollo 8 was out of range of the space agency's three deep-space tracking antennas—in California, Spain and Australia.

This was 10 minutes before the spacecraft's 20,500-pound-thrust main rocket was supposed to fire, slowing them down and dropping them into lunar orbit. The rocket is situated in the aft end of the spacecraft's 22-foot-long equipment unit called the service module. The forward crew compartment, the command module, is only 11 feet long.

ENGINE FIRES
ON SCHEDULE
If the engine failed to fire, the astronauts would merely loop around the moon's back side without going into orbit, and then whip back to earth.

But the engine ignited on schedule, at 4:59 A.M., and fired slightly more than four minutes. The engine was pointing toward the moon at an angle so that the firing acted as an explosive brake, slowing the spacecraft from a speed of 5,758 miles an hour to 3,643 miles an hour.

It was 20 minutes more before flight controllers here could know if they had an orbiting spacecraft. They waited in tense silence.

Then came a trickle of data indicating that the spacecraft was emerging and working well. Finally, a long minute later, there was a crackle of sound over the voice communication circuit.

Captain Lovell was talking. He was ever so matter of fact, the pilot first, leaving any poetry for later.

"Go ahead, Houston, Apollo 8," Captain Lovell said. "Burn complete. Our orbit is 169.1 by 60.5."

HAPPY TO GET MESSAGE
Amid the jubilation from the control room, Major Carr acknowledged the message:

"Apollo 8, this is Houston. Roger, 169.1 by 60.5. Good to hear your voice."

The numbers were the altitude of their moon orbit given in nautical miles. It translates to about 194.5 statute miles at the highest point, which would be on the front of the moon, and 69.6 miles at the low point, on the back side.

Flight controllers and the astronauts always deal in nautical miles. These figures are translated by reporters into statute miles.

As the astronauts emerged from around the eastern edge of the moon, traveling westward near the equator, the sun was shining high overhead.

Because of its slow rotation, the moon's daytimes and night-times both last 14 days. Most of the moon's back side and the east-ern edge of the side facing earth are now in sunlight. Much of the center part of the moon's face is partly illuminated now by the earth shine.

The astronauts' first concern was not the moon but a radiator in the spacecraft's cooling system. All the water had evaporated, and had to be replenished.

Then the astronauts looked down to see the crater-scarred moon.

One of the first major lunar features they spotted was the crater Langrenus, one of many craters with peaks rising from the center of their floors. They next flew over the broad plain called the Sea of Fertility.

When asked by ground controllers what "the old moon looks like," Captain Lovell began describing the sight unfolding below:

"The moon is essentially gray, no color. Looks like plaster of Paris or sort of grayish beach sand. We can see quite a bit of detail.

"The Sea of Fertility doesn't stand out as well here as it does back on earth. There's not as much contrast between that and the surrounding craters. The craters are all rounded off. There's quite a few of 'em. Some of them are newer. Many of them look like—especially the round ones—look like they were hit by meteorites or projectiles of some sort.

"Langrenus is quite a huge crater. It's got a central cone to it. The walls of the crater are terraced, about six or seven different terraces on the way down."

SOME "OLD FRIENDS" SEEN

Captain Lovell went on to describe two craters in the Sea of Fertility—his "old friends" Mess-ier and Pickering. He saw rays of light material extending out from Pickering's rim.

"Now we're coming upon the craters Colombo and Guten-berg," Major Anders said. "We can see the long parallel faults of Gaudibert, and a run through the mare [sea] material right into the highland material."

Faults are cracks in the lunar surface produced by stresses of unknown origin.

By then, Apollo 8 had passed over much of the daytime area of the moon and was reaching the Sea of Tranquility, an even broader plain on the right side of the moon, as seen from earth.

With the sun lower, close to the horizon, the astronauts were able to make out more details, especially enhancing their percep-tion of depth and height on the lunar surface.

This was the way they want-ed it. For on the Sea of Tranquil-ity lies one of the five sites being considered for the manned lunar landing planned for next year. The primary purpose of the Apol-lo 8 mission is to take detailed pictures of the area to help future astronauts steer to their landing.

"It's about impossible to miss," Captain Lovell assured flight controllers. "Very easy to pick out."

The spacecraft then flew over the terminator—the point where daylight changes to darkness. The view in that area, they reported, was quite sharper.

But beyond, even with the earthshine, it became more and more difficult to make out any landmarks on the surface.

After moving around the back side and reappearing in their second orbit, the astronauts aimed their 4.5-pound television camera on the moon and trans-mitted their first pictures. This began at 7:29 A.M.

At first the light was too bright, with the sun directly overhead. The first crater they looked down on was an unnamed one they called Brand, after Vince D. Brand. He is an astronaut acting as capsule communicator during the night shift.

Throughout their orbit the astronauts called many of the small unnamed craters on the back side by the names of friends, associates and themselves. The craters Borman, Lovell and Anders lay just south of the equator near where the back of the moon ends and the front begins.

Apollo officials said the crater names were in no way official, merely handy ways to identify some nameless features.

During the telecast, Major Anders, who handled the camera, described the scene below:

"The color of the moon looks like a very whitish gray, like dirty beach sand with lots of footprints in it. Some of these craters look like pickaxes striking concrete, creating a lot of fine haze dust."

Captain Lovell then reported seeing "a lot of what appears to be very small new craters that have these little white rays radiating from them."

The moon is believed to be about the same age as earth— some 4.5-billion to 5-billion years old. Since the moon has no atmosphere and no surface water, its face has not undergone the same erosion as the earth's has.

But through the ages it has been peppered with meteorites and rent with volcanic eruption, presumably the primary sources of the craters.

In the telecast the astronauts took pictures along a path running about 550 miles. A single picture usually covered an area some 175 miles wide.

After about 10 minutes, the astronauts signed off their telecast, promising to resume it on their ninth orbit. The show stopped as their spacecraft passed over Smyth's Sen and two prominent craters, Gilbert and Kuestner.

The astronauts complained again that three of the five spacecraft windows were hazy, clouding somewhat their view of the moon.

An analysis by engineers on the ground indicated that the problem probably lay in the rubberized caulking materials used to seal the windows' edges. They suspect that the material created the fogginess by giving off some traces of contaminating gases. The two clear windows were sealed by different substances.

However, the astronauts reported that the ice that had formed on the center window was melting. This came about because of the warming sunlight being reflected by the moon.

Passing over the Sea of Fertility for the second time, Major Anders took pictures with his 16-mm. movie camera. He described the sea as a darker brown than he had expected.

While in orbit the astronauts shot some 1,200 still pictures, many of them in color, with a 70-mm. Hasselblad camera, as well as movies and the television.

On one orbit Major Anders let the movie camera run for the completed two-hour revolution, taking pictures at one frame a second. He also took pictures of the terminator between day and night.

The subsequent orbits were fairly quiet. The astronauts ate and took a turn at some short naps. They continued to take color pictures, and also practiced sighting landmarks used for navigation.

From the tracking data, flight controllers have noticed that the spacecraft tended to "jiggle" when it flew over the famous crater Copernicus.

This was attributed to the fact, recently noted, that under the moon's surface there are scattered lumps of material of greater density. A slightly greater gravitational tug is exerted at these spots.

The unevenness, however, caused the astronauts no trouble. But the data are being analyzed carefully so that future moonfarers will know what to expect.

It was observed during the 10 orbits that the spacecraft's flight path underwent some slight but puzzling changes. Starting out in a circular orbit of 69.8 miles, Apollo 8 wound up sagging to nearly 68 miles at a low point and rising to nearly 73 miles at a high point.

Flight controllers could not immediately explain this tendency, which was being studied. It might be related to the moon's gravitation anomalies.

When night fell here and a bright quarter moon shone in the clear sky, mission control commented to Apollo 8 that "there is a beautiful moon out there."

Colonel Borman replied, "Now, we were just saying that there's a beautiful earth out there."

"It depends on your point of view," concluded the ground controller.

During the orbital voyage, Colonel Borman, the commander, did most of the piloting, while Captain Lovell navigated and Major Anders was cameraman.

At a news conference here, flight controllers were asked what emotional reaction the astronauts experienced on being the first men to fly around the moon and see it from up close. The radioed statements revealed little emotion.

To this Major Carr replied:

"I would certainly say it was one of jubilation, exultation and any other word I can think of that would be synonymous. This is something they have worked many, many months and weeks on. The more craters they saw and recognized, the more jubilant they became."

Textboxes

The following articles were adapted for use as textboxes throughout the book.

Pg. 10: Alden Whitman, "Ho Chi Minh Was Noted for Success in Blending Nationalism with Communism," *The New York Times*, September 4, 1969.

Pg. 26: Albin Krebs, "Lyndon Johnson: Controversial President," *The New York Times*, January 23, 1973.

Pg. 38: Murray Schumach, "Martin Luther King Jr.: Leader of Millions in Nonviolent Drive for Racial Justice," *The New York Times*, April 5, 1968.

Pg. 54: Alden Whitman, "De Gaulle Rallied France in War and Strove to Lead Her to Greatness," *The New York Times*, November 11, 1970.

Pg. 64: Alden Whitman, "Robert Francis Kennedy: Attorney General, Senator and Heir of the New Frontier," *The New York Times*, June 6, 1968.

Pg. 74: Richard Severo, "Alexander Dubcek, 70, dies in Prague." *The New York Times*, November 8, 1992.

Pg. 86: R. W. Apple, Jr., "The 37th President; Richard Nixon, 81, Dies," *The New York Times*, April 23, 1994.

Pg. 96: Wolfgang Saxon, "Díaz Ordaz, Ex-Mexican President Who Put Down Student Riots, Dies," *The New York Times*, July 16, 1969.

Articles

The following articles were reprinted in their entirety in the "Articles" section.

Pg. 113: Charles Mohr, "Street Clashes Go on in Vietnam, Foe Still Holds Parts of Cities," *The New York Times*, February 2, 1968.

Pg. 116: Tom Wicker, "Johnson Says He Won't Run." *The New York Times*, April 1, 1968.

Pg. 119: Earl Caldwell, "Martin Luther King Is Slain in Memphis," *The New York Times*, April 5, 1968.

Pg. 123: David Bird, "300 Protesting Columbia Students Barricade Office of College Dean," *The New York Times*, April 24, 1968.

Pg. 126: Lloyd Garrison, "Hundreds Are Hurt in Clashes in Paris," *The New York Times*, May 25, 1968.

Pg. 128: Warren Weaver, Jr., "Kennedy Shot and Gravely Wounded." *The New York Times*, June 5, 1968.

Pg. 130: Tad Szulc, "Czechoslovakia Invaded by Russians and Four Other Warsaw Pact Forces," *The New York Times*, August 21, 1968.

Pg. 132: J. Anthony Lukas, "Thousands March," *The New York Times*, August 30, 1968.

Pg. 136: Paul Montgomery, "At Least 20 Dead as Mexico Strife Reaches a Peak," *The New York Times*, October 3, 1968.

Pg. 138: John Noble Wilford, "3 Men Fly Around the Moon Only 70 Miles from Surface," *The New York Times*, December 25, 1968.

"I Feel Like I'm Fixin' to Die Rag" words and music by Joe McDonald © 1965, renewed 1993 by Alkatraz Corner Music Co., BMI. Used by permission.

INDEX

FURTHER READING

Branch, Taylor. *At Canaan's Edge, America in the King Years, 1965–68.* New York: Simon & Schuster, 2006.

Dallek, Robert. *Lyndon B. Johnson: Portrait of a President.* New York: Oxford University Press, 2005.

Judt, Tony. *Postwar: A History of Europe Since 1945.* New York: Penguin, 2005.

Kaiser, Charles. *1968 in America.* New York: Grove Press, 1988.

Karnow, Stanley. *Vietnam, a History.* New York: Viking Press, 1983.

Kurlansky, Mark. *1968, The Year That Rocked The World.* New York: Random House, 2005.

Ryback, Timothy. *Rock Around the Bloc.* New York: Oxford University Press, 1990.

Thomas, Evan. *Robert Kennedy: His Life.* New York: Simon & Schuster, 2002.

PHOTO CREDITS